THE LAST WALTZ

THE LAST WALTZ

THE STRAUSS DYNASTY
AND VIENNA

JOHN SUCHET

THOMAS DUNNE BOOKS

ST. MARTIN'S PRESS ⚏ NEW YORK

THOMAS DUNNE BOOKS.
An imprint of St. Martin's Press.

THE LAST WALTZ: THE STRAUSS DYNASTY AND VIENNA.
Copyright © 2015 by John Suchet. All rights reserved. Printed in Italy.
For information, address St. Martin's Press, 175 Fifth Avenue,
New York, N.Y. 10010

thomasdunnebooks.com
www.stmartins.com

Designed by James Collins

The Library of Congress Cataloging-in-Publication Data
is available upon request.

ISBN 978-1-250-09411-7 (hardcover)
ISBN 978-1-250-09410-0 (e-book)

St. Martin's Press books may be purchased for educational, business, or
promotional use. For information on bulk purchases, please contact the
Macmillan Corporate and Premium Sales Department at 1-800-221-7945,
extension 5442, or write to specialmarkets@macmillan.com.

First published in Great Britain in 2015 by Elliott and Thompson Limited

First U.S. Edition

10 9 8 7 6 5 4 3 2 1

Printed and bound in Italy by Printer Trento.

For Nula

Contents

Introduction

The name of Johann Strauss, and the sound of his music, are synonymous with Vienna. They are Vienna. Johann Strauss the Younger, the Waltz King, may have been dead for over a century, but there is not a night of the week when his music cannot be heard somewhere in Vienna. And wherever in the world it is heard, it is the image of the city of Vienna and of its river the Danube that are instantly conjured up.

So beautiful, melodious and instantly memorable are the pieces he wrote, that you could easily believe that he, his father and brothers – prolific and successful composers all – lived in perfect harmony, both musically and otherwise, and that the city of their birth was as peaceful and content as their music.

The truth was very different. The Strauss family was riven with tension, rivalry and jealousy. The founder of the dynasty, Johann Strauss senior, deserted his family. His three sons worked literally to the point of exhaustion – one killing himself through overwork, another constantly ill with the strain of composing, the third ultimately burning thousands of family manuscripts in a fit of jealousy.

And the Vienna in which they lived? A revolution on the streets brought to the throne an emperor who would lose his only son to suicide and his wife to murder. In the second half of the nineteenth century the once great Habsburg Empire would dwindle in power and influence, dwarfed by the might and militarism of Prussia.

Through it all the Viennese would drink champagne and waltz to the music of the Strauss dynasty, as they hurtled towards the First World War and oblivion.

This book tells the extraordinary story of the most prolific and popular family of composers in musical history, and of the turbulent city in which they lived.

Left

The cover of *By the Beautiful Blue Danube,* Johann Strauss the Younger's most popular work.

Chapter One
CITY OF DREAMS

There is a saying in Vienna: 'When one eye cries, the other one laughs.' Another has it that 'Things are desperate but not serious.'

Vienna is a city of contradictions, as the Viennese themselves know well, and you need look no further than its music to prove it.

The single most famous piece of music to emerge from Vienna, a piece that encapsulates the spirit of the city, that is heard without fail at every Vienna New Year's Day concert, that from the opening of shimmering violins says 'This is Vienna', is named for its river.

I can think of no other great capital city that has a universally known and loved piece of music named for its river. Not the Seine in Paris, the Thames in London, the Tiber in Rome, the Vltava in Prague,[1] the Spree in Berlin, the Vistula in Warsaw, the Moskva in Moscow.

But Vienna has *'By the Beautiful Blue Danube'*. And yet every river I have named runs through the centre of its city, *except* the Danube. The Danube skirts round the city of Vienna. For many hundreds of years the traveller arriving by boat in Vienna had quite an onward journey to reach the centre of the city. It was true when Johann Strauss wrote his famous waltz, and it is true today.

How then did this great city come to be indelibly identified with its river through music, a river that does not even touch it? Just one of the many contradictions of Vienna.

---

[1] Perhaps the closest, though 'Vltava' is the second of six symphonic poems which make up Smetana's *Ma Vlast* ('My Homeland').

For the explanation behind its wealth of contradictions, take a look at a map of mainland Europe. Vienna sits pretty much at the centre of the landmass. From the earliest times travellers passed through Vienna, from the north, south, east and west, bringing with them their language, customs, ideas and sounds. Inevitably many never left.

During the whole of the nineteenth century, fewer than half of those living in Vienna were Viennese by birth. Not many years before Johann Strauss II was born in 1825, a visitor to Vienna wrote:

> *A feast for the eyes here is the variety of national costumes from different countries … Here you can meet the Hungarian striding swiftly with his close-fitting trousers reaching almost to his ankles and his long pigtail, or the round-headed Pole with his monkish haircut and flowing sleeves … Armenians, Romanians and Moldavians with their half-Oriental costumes … Serbians with their twisted moustaches occupy a whole street – The Greeks in their wide heavy dress can be seen in hordes smoking their long-stemmed pipes in the coffee houses … Bearded Muslims in yellow mules with their broad murderous knives in their belts … Polish Jews all swathed in black, their faces bearded and their hair all twisted in knots … Bohemian peasants with their long boots … Hungarian and Transylvanian wagoners with sheepskin greatcoats, Croats with black tubs balanced on their heads – they all provide entertaining accents in the general throng.*

The same visitor wrote that the native languages ('native' not 'foreign'!) of the Austrian empire were German, Latin, French, Italian, Hungarian, Bohemian, Polish, Flemish, Greek, Turkish, Illyrian, Croatian, Slavic, Romanian and Romany.

"Of all the customs and exotica travellers brought with them, none embedded itself more in the fabric of Vienna than music."

Of all the customs and exotica travellers brought with them,
none embedded itself more in the culture – the very fabric – of
Vienna than music.

> *Here bassoonists and clarinettists are as plentiful as blackberries … no*
> *place of refreshment, from the highest to the lowest, is without music …*
> *one cannot enter any fashionable house without hearing a duet, or trio, or*
> *finale from one of the Italian operas currently the rage … even shopkeep-*
> *ers and cellar-hands whistle arias.*

Why might this be? First, and most obviously, because of all the arts
music is the most accessible and influential. Foreigners have long
played their music in the streets of Vienna, and the Viennese have
listened enthralled.[2] But there is another, more sinister, reason.

In the dying decade of the eighteenth century, Vienna – capital of the Holy Roman Empire, seat of the Holy Roman Emperor,
head of the mighty House of Habsburg – was a city living in an atmosphere of increasing fear and suspicion. Just a few hundred miles

---

[2] It happens to this day. On my last visit to Vienna, just a couple of years ago, I
stood in a crowd listening to street musicians playing folk music from the Andes.

to the north-west, a rampaging mob had brought down the French monarchy, leading first the king, then his queen, to the scaffold, and was now in the process of trying to obliterate an entire social class.

No other city in Continental Europe was as class conscious, as socially structured, as Vienna, and no other monarchy as powerful or autocratic as the Habsburgs. If the British monarchy – and people – had at least a narrow but forbiddingly protective stretch of water to safeguard them, then Vienna, its monarchy and its aristocracy, were obvious first targets if the new French rulers decided to export their revolution by means of the French Revolutionary Army under their brilliant young commander Napoleon Bonaparte.

Austria's iron-willed chancellor, Klemens von Metternich, had the answer. He simply brought the shutters down on Europe's most vibrant city. A network of spies was created; any activity remotely seditious was immediately reported; people of all classes thought before they spoke, and when they did speak they took great care over what they said. Anything else was simply too dangerous.

Which, in a nutshell, is how Vienna came to be Europe's capital city of music. If words are not safe, what is? Music. Who can say that a folk band in a tavern, a café, or on a street corner, is fomenting dissent? And so Europe's musicians flocked to Vienna. A roll-call of composers who lived or worked in Vienna, or merely visited it in the century and a half to 1900, is like a recitation of some of the greatest names in music: Haydn, Mozart, Beethoven, Schubert, Mendelssohn, Schumann, Wagner, Johann Strauss II, Bruckner, Brahms, Mahler – and they are only the best known.

Yet, of those great names, only two were actually Viennese, born in Vienna. Franz Schubert and Johann Strauss. And of these two, one alone can be said to encapsulate Vienna in his music – the zest, sounds, rhythms, excitement, laughter, gaiety and sadness.

The music of Johann Strauss does not just encapsulate the contradictions of Vienna; it provides an explanation for them and in so doing it supersedes them. The most famous couplet of his best-loved operetta, *Die Fledermaus*, reads: 'Happy is he who is able to forget what he cannot change.'[3] A more succinct summation of the Viennese character – and indeed for those Viennese not naturally blessed with

---

[3] 'Glücklich ist wer vergisst, was doch nicht zu ändern ist.'

it one they were able to adopt – is hard to find. To think of Johann Strauss, to listen to his music, is to think of Vienna and hear its sounds.

But it was a long and dangerous journey from the carefree days described by that earlier traveller to the era of Strauss, the waltz and champagne. In between came nearly four decades of fear and tension.

Vienna has always been something of a frontier city. In Metternich's time it was a pointed joke to say that on the other side of the city's most easterly tollgate the Orient began. A century and a half later Vienna was the last city in the West before the barbed wire and sentry posts marked the beginning of communist Eastern Europe. Buildings that once looked out over the Hungarian plain, from where the Ottoman army came to besiege Vienna, now looked out over a land whose people were shut off from the West on pain of death.[4]

Vienna, then, has been well acquainted with danger and intrigue. The decades between the Congress of Vienna in 1814, which attempted to redraw the post-Napoleonic map of Europe, and the revolutions of 1848 that swept away the old order, were to stamp themselves indelibly on the Viennese character. During those long years the city, and its people, turned in on themselves.

The period is known to us as the Biedermeier era, and it introduced a particular word to the lexicon: *'Gemütlichkeit'*, a word that cannot be translated into a single English equivalent. It is a state of mind that is cheerful, happy and unworried, accepting of what life may bring.

A close approximation of the meaning of *'Gemütlichkeit'* in English would be a sort of comfortableness, cosiness, even amiability. Yet how could such a mood exist in a city of fear? The answer is simple. It existed in the comfort of your own home – and only there.

That is where the name 'Biedermeier' comes in. It derived originally from a series of humorous poems depicting a comically naive schoolteacher by the name of Papa Biedermeier. By a series of mutations, the name came to describe the comfort and safety of your own home in a city where talk in a public place was dangerous.

In those tense years the Viennese simply stayed at home, where they knew they would be safe, or visited the homes of close friends and associates. Aristocrats, patrons of the arts, held soirées in their palaces. For the upper classes it was a salon life replete with culture.

---

[4] The 1949 film *The Third Man* perfectly portrays Vienna, the frontier city.

To a degree this was simply an extension of how it had always been. A generation earlier the young Beethoven had made his name in the salons of the nobility, who were stunned at his extraordinary virtuosity and his ability to improvise on the piano. Franz Schubert entertained friends at home with such regularity that the evenings were known as Schubertiades.

Then, in 1825, Johann Strauss the Younger was born – right in the middle of the Biedermeier era, he grew up under its influence. His music is inseparable from the period.

So how does the Strauss dynasty fit into this rich and complex tapestry? How did the music of a father and his three sons come to encapsulate the spirit of that contradictory city so perfectly?

On 14 March 1804 a child born in a small tavern on the banks of the Danube in the run-down Viennese suburb of Leopoldstadt was given the name Johann. His father, who managed the tavern, was

Franz Strauss. Thanks to this child the name Strauss would forever be linked to music and the Viennese waltz.

It was a propitious time for a musician to be born. The Irish tenor Michael Kelly, visiting Vienna twenty years earlier, where he befriended Mozart, spoke of a city where it seemed the whole populace danced. There were dance halls in all the suburbs, and most taverns had a resident band and a space for dancing.

Taking their cue from the victorious revolutionaries in Paris, the stately dances that had been the province of the aristocracy – the minuet, the allemande, the bourrée – were quickly replaced by the stamping and whirling dances that had been familiar in village taverns across southern Germany for generations, the *'Ländler'*.[5]

With increasing boat travel east along the Danube, across Bavaria and into Austria, it was not long before the bucolic rhythms and sounds reached Europe's most sophisticated city, Vienna. They were soon taken up by resident bands in the city's dance halls and taverns, and the common populace delighted in the new entertainment, beer mugs overflowing, feet stamping.

There was a unique feature that set these dances apart from the dances of the nobility. The man and woman faced each other, arms entwined, bodies clasped tightly. In other words they danced as a couple, as opposed to dancing partners facing mostly in the same direction, their hands possibly touching lightly in the air.

In the wake of the French Revolution there was a new feeling of freedom and release among the lower social classes in aristocratic Vienna. It would not last, of course, once Metternich took matters in hand, but in the closing decade of the eighteenth century and the opening decade of the nineteenth, for the first time music, fashion and tastes in general permeated up the social scale rather than down.

They did not survive the transition entirely intact, however. The polished wooden floors of aristocratic salons, so suited to the leather-soled shoes of the aristocracy, might have been the perfect surface on which to dance the minuet, but they were entirely unsuited to the *Ländler* and the boots and clogs in which they were normally danced.

And so, over a remarkably short period of time, the stomp developed into a slide, the hobnail gave way to leather. The new dance

---

[5] 'Of the country', or 'rural'.

Left

Emperor Franz Josef I dancing the waltz at the annual Viennese Ball.

Right

Johnann Strauss the Elder, founder of the most popular and prolific musical dynasty in history.

was in three-four time, the man holding the woman close, one hand clasping hers, the other pressing her body to his. Faces could be close, cheeks could touch, lips brush lightly. The waltz was born.[6] This was the sound, the rhythm, that young Johann listened to from his earliest years, that he grew up hearing. It was said that as a child he would creep down from his bedroom and hide under tables so he could hear the music and watch the couples dance.

It was as well he had music as a distraction, because his early years were fraught with sadness. When he was just seven years old, his mother died from fever. His father remarried, but five years later his body was found floating in the river that ran swiftly past the tavern he managed. It was never established whether he drowned accidentally or committed suicide.

Johann's father left a debt-ridden estate and it was no surprise that his stepmother apprenticed the boy months later to a tailor, who very soon passed him on to a bookbinder. The boy, now thirteen, hated this apprenticeship, complaining years later that his whole boyhood stank of glue.

But there was salvation. Exactly how Johann Strauss came into possession of a cheap Bavarian violin made of poor-quality wood is not known. It is possible his new stepfather – by all accounts a kindly man – gave it to him. It is just as likely it was abandoned by an itinerant musician after a night's drinking. What is certain, however, is that it swiftly became the boy's most treasured possession.[7]

He took to it like a duck to water. We know he received violin lessons, though not from whom, and this preoccupation with music ran alongside his bookbinding apprenticeship. At the age of just fifteen, possibly even younger, he landed a place in the highly popular dance orchestra led by violinist and conductor Michael Pamer. This impressed his stepfather enough to allow him to leave the smell of glue behind to pursue a career as musician.[8]

---

[6] From the verb *'walzen'*, 'to turn'.

[7] I would like to believe the story that when the tone of the fiddle was too dry and thin, Johann would pour beer into it to give a more moist, and consequently sentimental, tone.

[8] It's possible he actually played viola in the orchestra, which would be even more impressive.

Gedr. bei L.Förster.   Federzeichnung v. Berndt.

Pamer was an interesting character. Forced to give up the violin because of an injury to his left index finger, he made up for it with monumental intakes of beer – while conducting. Pamer's showpiece was a number to which he gave the nickname *'Blessed Memories of Hütteldorf Beer'*, pausing to drink a mugful in honour of the memory after each piece. The audience, entering into the game, regularly called for as many as twenty encores, resulting in Pamer collapsing in a heap in front of the orchestra and conducting on his back.

It is surely not too fanciful to imagine a young and impressionable Johann Strauss, sitting in the orchestra and observing closely how extroversion and showmanship can involve an audience more closely in music making, even if this particular example was somewhat extreme.

There was another young member of the violin section in Pamer's orchestra, three years older than Johann, by the name of Joseph Lanner. The two must have formed a friendship, because it was not long before both had resigned from the orchestra and were working together. Lanner had been the first to leave, setting up his own trio with two friends, soon to be joined by Strauss, the trio becoming a quartet. Johann and Joseph formed a close bond, even sharing lodgings.

These two highly talented violinists soon attracted attention, not least because they were such opposites. 'Black Schani' (Strauss) was olive-skinned with dark wavy hair, described by the Viennese in local dialect as 'peppery', 'vibrant', even 'sharp-tongued'. 'Blond Peppi' (Lanner) by contrast was 'mild', 'smooth', 'silken'.

That applied to their music too, because what set these two apart from the many other musicians playing in orchestras and bands was that both began to compose. Lanner, as the older and more experienced, was the more productive of the two. Although – in an uncanny prescience of what would happen a generation later to an as yet unborn Johann Strauss the Younger – the strain of rehearsing, conducting, arranging and composing began to take a toll on Lanner's health.

Lanner, the driving force in the partnership, had expanded his quartet to a small string orchestra, and when that proved insufficient to handle the ever increasing workload, formed a second orchestra. He appointed his friend and partner, Johann Strauss, as 'vice-conductor' of this orchestra.

Left

Joseph Lanner, close friend and later bitter rival of Johann Strauss the Elder.

It proved to be a mistake – for Lanner. The young Johann Strauss, just turned twenty-one, had found his calling. Suddenly his boundless energy, his hitherto untapped organisational skills, his natural authority, the ability to lead, set him apart. Once Lanner asked him to come up swiftly with a set of waltzes for an event that same evening – he was too unwell to do it himself. Just once and never again. It was a triumph for Strauss.

There was no holding him. He did more than just compose. He arranged pieces by other composers, hired the musicians, and booked venues. But what impressed the ever growing audiences most of all was that Johann Strauss led the orchestra from the violin. This was not unknown in Vienna, or in taverns along the Danube. But usually the violinist would stand in front of a small handful of musicians, his part no more or less important than theirs. Strauss did more than just play or accompany. He led. No one doubted who was in charge, or who took the bows at the end.

The young man developed a certain swagger, as his name began to be talked of around town. It was not long before Strauss realised he had the skills, and the public recognition, to forge a career on his own. The friend and colleague who had given him his break was now superfluous, if not actually a hindrance. He went to Lanner and told him he planned a solo career. Lanner knew full well what he was losing and the discussions, which took place over a number of days, became increasingly heated. Matters reached a head at a concert the two men gave together at a large ballroom by the name of Zum Bock ('At the Ram').

In the early hours of the morning, with the concert over and large quantities of alcohol consumed, the two men – so legend has it – came to blows. Instruments were damaged and furniture was smashed. There was no going back. It was a parting of the ways, which Lanner commemorated in his *'Trennungswalzer'* ('Separation Waltz').[9]

Johann Strauss was on his own. Well, not entirely. In the first place he took fourteen of Lanner's best musicians with him, which allowed him to put together a serviceable orchestra from the start. Secondly, and of considerably more importance to musical history, he had met a young woman and fallen in love.

Anna Streim was the daughter of the landlord of Zum roten Hahn ('At the Red Rooster'), a tavern in a suburb of Vienna. Johann wooed and won Anna, and on 11 July 1825 the couple were married. Johann was twenty-one, his bride two years older. Less than four months later, on 25 October 1825, Anna gave birth. The baby was a boy, and he was named after his father. This was the Johann Strauss who would go on to eclipse his father as a musician, and become the best-loved, most prolific, internationally lauded composer that the city of Vienna had ever – or would ever – produce.

---

[9] There is no documentary evidence of the fracas, but why should there be? Certainly it was the talk of Vienna within a very short time, and even if an element of exaggeration has crept in, there is no doubt the two young men parted acrimoniously.

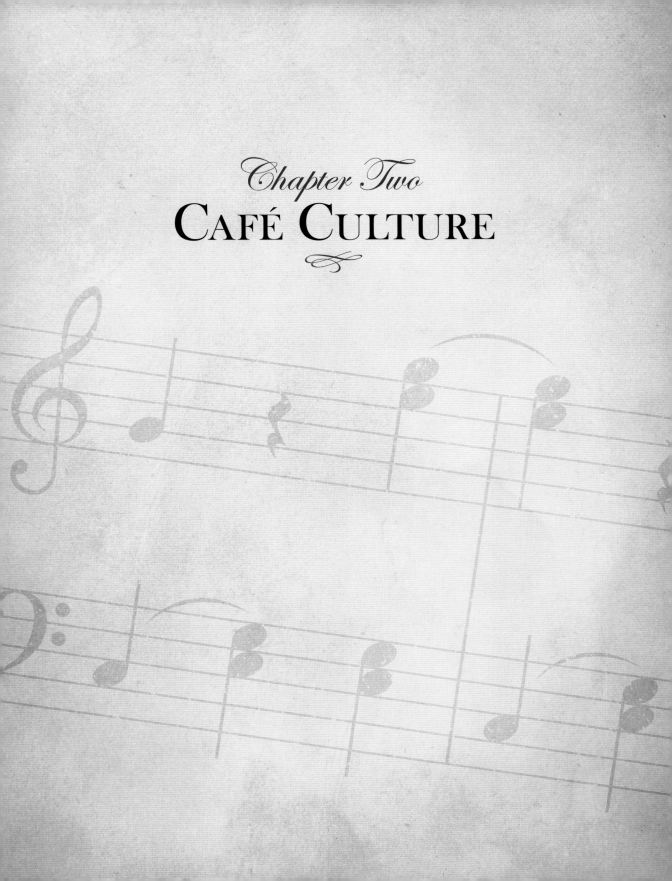

Chapter Two
CAFÉ CULTURE

*I*f Vienna was Europe's capital city of music, it was also — and still is — the European capital of the café. It is possible there was a café in Oxford, or Venice, earlier than in Vienna, but it was in the Habsburg capital that the café or coffee house firmly took root and became a way of life. The reason for this is not hard to find. The Habsburg empire traded closely with the Ottoman empire, and the coffee bean so prevalent in Istanbul quickly made its way to Vienna, where it was in abundant supply. Cafés soon proliferated in the city and became the favoured places to meet, gossip and listen to local bands.

But there is a much more interesting and engaging explanation of how Vienna came to be the café capital of Europe, and it is one known to the Viennese today, and certainly to most Viennese of earlier centuries, in particular to musicians for whom the café, and later the dance hall, were to provide so many new venues for their work. It is, of course, a legend, and as such has become embroidered over the passage of time, but a legend becomes so only because it is based on truth, and this one has more than a ring of truth about it.

Every legend has a hero, and the name of this one is Georg Franz Kolschitzky.[10] A Polish street trader, Kolschitzky had spent some years travelling and trading in Turkey and so became fluent in Turkish and familiar with Turkish customs and traditions. At one time he had served as translator in the Turkish army. He was therefore the right man in the right place when the Turks, for the second

---

[10] Variously Kolschitzky, Koltschitzki, Kulczycki.

time in a century and a half, sent a huge army west with the aim of conquering Europe and destroying Christendom. The Crusades in reverse, as it were. After the first failed attempt under Suleiman the Magnificent, when the siege was broken by the Viennese, a massive defensive wall – the Bastei – had been built around the city with the explicit aim of keeping out any later attempt.

Now, in 1683, that wall threatened to prove more of a hindrance than a help. An army of 300,000 Turks simply set up camp outside it, prevented any movement of supplies through its ten gates, and waited for the Viennese, holed up inside, to surrender before they starved. The Glacis, the expanse of green that lay beyond the wall, bristled with tents, and the air was filled with smoke and the exotic aromas of Levantine spices.

The commander of the meagre forces inside the city wall, Count Starhemberg, was aware that help, of a kind, was at hand. The Duke of Lorraine was camped on the other side of the Danube with a force of just 33,000 men – no match for the Turks. But King Jan Sobieski of Poland had left Warsaw and was gathering forces as he marched south-west to Vienna. If and when Sobieski and Lorraine could join forces, there was the faint hope that the Turks could be defeated and the siege lifted.

The situation inside the city wall was becoming desperate. Starhemberg knew time was short and it was imperative to get word out to Lorraine of just how serious things were, and how quickly help was needed. Several times he dispatched envoys with orders to get through enemy lines, only to see their bodies hanging outside the city wall days later as a warning and deterrent.

Enter the man who could speak fluent Turkish, understood Turkish ways, and could – with a measure of good fortune – pass himself off as one of the enemy. Could Kolschitzky succeed where others had failed?

On 13 August he left the city and walked through the Turkish encampment, passing himself off as a trader from Belgrade. So successful was he that at one point he was captured by locals in the little village of Kahlenberg and only managed to persuade them he was not one of the enemy by speaking to them in a Viennese dialect no one who was not Viennese could possibly know.

Kolschitzky reached Lorraine safely. A rocket was fired off to signify this, and a rocket was fired from the roof of St Stephen's

Cathedral in the city in acknowledgement. Kolschitzky apprised Lorraine of the dire situation inside the city wall and the desperate need for action. Lorraine dispatched couriers to Sobieski and other European leaders, urging them to send forces to Vienna at maximum speed, warning that otherwise Vienna would be lost, leaving Europe at the mercy of the Muslim horde.

His task complete, Kolschitzky made the dangerous return journey to the besieged city. He came even closer to having his cover blown on this return trip, he later said, and had to call on every ounce of skill and deception that he possessed. Against all the odds he arrived safely back in Vienna on 17 August.

Less than a month later a large relief force made up of Poles, Germans, Austrians and several other European nationalities gathered on the summit of Mount Kahlenberg, at the extreme eastern end of the Vienna woods, overlooking the city. At midnight on 11 September the troops were blessed in an outdoor mass, and at dawn on the 12th, led by the Polish king, they charged down the hillside straight into the Turkish camp.

A defensive line of Turkish trenches to the north-west of the city was quickly overwhelmed,[11] and after a fierce but one-sided battle the Turks were routed. They fled in disarray, unable even to dismantle their tents or pack up goods and equipment. It was the last attempt by a Turkish army to invade Europe.

King Jan Sobieski of Poland became an instant hero across Europe, to this day revered by Poles who will tell you that their king saved Christendom and that had it not been for him Europe would now be Muslim. Kolschitzky became an instant hero in Vienna and a grateful Emperor Leopold asked him to choose a reward from the bounty the Turks had left behind.

And what exactly had the Turks left behind? The inventory included 25,000 tents, 10,000 oxen, 5,000 camels, 100,000 bushels of grain, a huge quantity of gold, and hundreds of sacks filled with green beans that no one in Vienna had seen before or knew what use to make of them. No one except Kolschitzky, who from his time in Istanbul knew instantly that they were coffee beans. He asked the

Georg Franz Kolschitzky, saviour of Vienna and founder of the Viennese café.

---

[11] On the site today stands a large park called the Türkenschanzpark, 'Turkish trench park'.

Right

Monument to
Kolschitzky in Vienna,
sculpted by Emanuel
Pendl, showing him
serving coffee, on the
corner of the street
named after him.

emperor for the sacks and their contents, and permission to open an establishment serving the drink he would make from the beans, known as coffee. The emperor was only too pleased to oblige.

Thus Vienna acquired its first coffee house, or café, and the Viennese first fell in love with the drink that would come to epitomise them. Well, not quite that easily. For, as the legend goes, the drink that Kolschitzky first brewed was much too bitter for Viennese tastes and it failed to catch on.

Then someone suggested to Kolschitzky that he should add milk. This improved matters considerably, but still he failed to make a success of the venture. Another suggestion: why don't you use cream instead of milk, and whip it?

The rest, as they say, is history. Now it might well be that these last few details have accrued something in the telling, but the fact remains that to this day there is a street in Vienna named after Georg Franz Kolschitzky, the Kolschitzkygasse, and on the corner of it, on the first floor, is a statue of Kolschitzky in Turkish garb, holding a tray with coffee cups, erected by a grateful Coffee Makers Guild of Vienna.

To say that Kolschitzky started something is an understatement. Cafés proliferated across the city. By the 1830s there were eighty coffee houses in the city centre, and at least fifty more in the suburbs. This coincided with an equally extensive proliferation of dance halls in Vienna. As a new century dawned there were the beginnings of mechanical industry that within a few decades would revolutionise people's lives. There was more wealth than ever before, and with it the Viennese demanded more entertainment, more opportunity for relaxation.

That meant music, and music meant dancing. Coffee houses became ever more numerous, and dance halls – taking their cue from Paris – became more and more luxurious. Elaborate chandeliers hung from the ceiling, a thousand wax candles glittering in them. In the centre of one hall, the Apollo Palace, sat an immense rock from which springs flowed out in tumbling cascades, down into large tanks filled with live fish.

But the most sensational import from the French capital was wooden parquet flooring, never before seen in Vienna. What could be better for the new dance that was swiftly becoming a craze? The waltz was taking hold in Vienna at just the time the young Johann

Strauss I was weighing up the possibilities of a solo career. The style and rhythms of the music came naturally to him. He played it and he wrote it, and the Viennese delighted in it.

In a remarkable confluence of increased sophistication, public taste, a desire for change, and the move into a new century, the waltz took hold in Vienna, never to leave it. It could not have been a better moment for a certain young musician to strike out on his own, form his own orchestra, experiment with his own compositions, see if he could make a name for himself.

Johann Strauss the Elder was on his way.

But things were not easy. Johann Strauss had a growing family, mouths to feed. A second son, Josef, was born less than two years after Johann junior, followed by two girls, Anna and Therese, again at two-yearly intervals. A fifth child lived only ten months, and in March 1835 the couple's sixth and last child, Eduard, was born. A growing family necessitated more living space and they moved house four times in under ten years, each time to more expensive accommodation.

It meant Johann senior had to work hard, and this he certainly did. Compositions poured from him. By the time of his first real success, the '*Sperls Fest-Walzer*', a piece he composed to celebrate his debut at Vienna's newest and most prestigious dance hall, the Sperl, he had already composed nearly thirty pieces, not just waltzes but gallops as well.

As his fame grew, musicians clamoured to work with him, and he was impressing some rather big names in the world of music. Writing with characteristic hyperbole, a certain Richard Wagner, who visited Vienna in the summer of 1832, said:

> *I shall never forget the extraordinary playing of Johann Strauss, who … made the audience almost frantic with delight. At the beginning of a new waltz this demon of the Viennese musical spirit shook like a Pythian princess on the tripod, and veritable groans of ecstasy which, without doubt, were more due to his music than to the drinks in which the audience had indulged, raised their worship for the magic violinist to almost bewildering heights of frenzy.*

Strauss had learned well from the flamboyance of Michael Pamer. Frédéric Chopin too, then only twenty-one, noted a year earlier that 'Lanner, Strauss and their waltzes obscure everything'.

But Johann Strauss was soon to leave Lanner far behind, as word of the magic that this remarkable young musician seemed to instil in audiences, and the flamboyance with which he led his orchestra from the violin – 'His own limbs no longer belong to him when the desert storm of his waltz is let loose, his fiddle bow dances with his arms, the melody waves champagne glasses in his face,' wrote one reveller after an evening at the Sperl – spread beyond his home city of Vienna.

It was not long before Johann Strauss and his orchestra took to the road. A short trip down the Danube led to a sparkling performance in Pest – 'Herr Strauss triumphed … with the first stroke of his bow' – and after several more months of concerts and balls in

Above

Strauss's house on Lerchenfelder Strasse, where Johann Strauss the Younger was born.

Vienna, Strauss received an extraordinary invitation to travel with his orchestra to Berlin.

Berlin, capital of Prussia, formal, correct, proper, militaristic, as far removed from the easy-going culture of Vienna several hundred miles to the south as it was possible to be. But this was no ordinary invitation. Strauss found himself performing before the King of Prussia at his court, and his highly distinguished guests the Tsar and Empress of Russia.

So enthralled were the royal personages that the king rewarded Strauss handsomely with a fee so large it was packed in a satchel, and the tsar presented him with a golden snuffbox. A normally sober-minded and restrained Berlin newspaper critic wrote, 'Look at little Strauss. He has turned all our good citizens into Viennese.' Another was so overwhelmed that he seemed to lose control of his critical faculties:

> *I am so happy, so joyful, so glad that I want to kiss the heavens with their stars; so recklessly, deliriously happy that I want to embrace the whole world and press it to my heart! And why? Because I have heard him! I have heard Johann Strauss!*

On the return journey to Vienna, Strauss and his orchestra performed in Leipzig, Dresden and Prague. Months later they left on another tour – a three-month trip through southern Germany, performing forty concerts in nineteen different towns. The following year saw their most extensive and ambitious tour to date. It lasted almost four months and took them back to Prague and Leipzig, then to Hanover and Hamburg, from there to Amsterdam, Rotterdam, Düsseldorf, Cologne and Brussels, and finally back to Vienna to arrive the day before New Year's Eve, 1835.

Everywhere the orchestra played the audience seemed to relish a feeling of liberation, as if they had at last been given permission to get up and dance, to smile and laugh, sing and shout, drink and dance their troubles away. Johann Strauss had struck a chord, literally.

As well as the unique sight – certainly outside Vienna – of seeing Strauss leading from the violin, swaying in time to the music, his waving bow a thousand times more expressive than a conductor's baton, there was something else that set Johann Strauss apart. He would frequently mark a visit to a town or city by composing

"Everywhere they played the audience seemed to relish a feeling of liberation, as if they were at last given permission to get up and dance."

a new piece in its honour, and performing it before a suitably flattered audience.

For that first visit to Pest, he composed *'Emlek Pestre – Erinnerung an Pesth'* ('Memory of Pest'), and for Berlin *'Erinnerung an Berlin'* ('Memory of Berlin'). By the time he returned to Vienna at the end of 1835 he had composed more than eighty pieces; more than eighty opus numbers to his name. Vienna had not seen anything like it. Johann Strauss, barely turned thirty years of age, was a phenomenon.

But his new-found fame was coming at a price. On his return from Pest – and that was before Berlin and the other towns and cities – Strauss wrote to his doctor, 'My left arm is very strained, which I attribute to my playing the violin, which hurts me.' Not a good omen for the future. There was another problem too, and one he could do nothing about. Despite the extraordinary reviews and seemingly ubiquitous adulation, Strauss's music was not meeting with universal approval. In certain sectors of Protestant northern Germany there was open hostility towards the waltz, which was, in the eyes of these strict moralists, an infestation from the Catholic south.

The dance was condemned as 'an incitement to sinful passion', and decried as 'demoralising and lewd'. Protestant zealots recruited the medical profession to their side and published a treatise entitled *Proof That the Waltz is a Main Cause of the Weakness of Body and Mind of Our Generation*.[12] They could point to actual harm caused by the waltz. Some dancers had fainted due to over-exertion and there had even been reports of deaths. These sad occurrences had affected men more than women, a sure sign – as the opposition were careful to avoid saying – of enjoyment and indulgence taken to extreme.

These were not just a small number of disaffected Protestants preaching to deaf ears. In some towns they succeeded in having their opposition to the waltz enshrined in law on the grounds that it was inimical to health. In others, including cities as important as Magdeburg and Frankfurt, police edicts were issued against the 'improper

---

[12] *Beweis, dass der Walzer eine Hauptquelle der Schwäche des Körpers und des Geistes unserer Generation sey.*

and horrible turning of women by men', particularly if done in such a manner as 'to make skirts fly up and reveal too much'.

Disaffection with the waltz, though, could not last. It was impossible to withstand the avalanche of popularity and enthusiasm that swept not just Austria and Germany but beyond their borders and across Europe. Johann Strauss and his orchestra were growing more popular internationally by the day, and the name of Johann Strauss was fast becoming the best-loved musical name in Europe. What could possibly go wrong? The answer is a lot. Nothing to do with music. It was much nearer home than that, and it was to have a profound effect on the Strausses of the next generation.

Chapter Three
CONQUERING PARIS

$\mathcal{L}$ife 'on the road' held many attractions for Johann Strauss I, not least the perfect justification to absent himself from a naturally disorganised household with five children ranging, at the end of 1835, from ten years of age to twelve months.

There were also all the temptations open to a young, highly attractive man, spending every night away from home. I have already noted Strauss's unusual complexion, compared to the typically blond Viennese Joseph Lanner. Strauss's paternal grandparents were both Jewish, and he had inherited their dark complexion.[13] He had lustrous black wavy hair and there are numerous descriptions of his sparkling eyes, dazzling good looks and magnetic personality.

There was no shortage of female admirers at his concerts, and Strauss was not reluctant to benefit from what was on offer. There is no doubt word got back to Anna in Vienna, and she seems to have accepted his transgressions as a price to be paid for a successful and lucrative career, which had allowed the family to move into a spacious and elegant house in a smart area of the city. That changed, though, when Anna received information that suggested that one liaison had become rather more permanent than the others, that Johann in fact had a mistress, not in some distant town, but in Vienna itself.

---

[13] This led to one of the most bizarre acts of documentary falsification of the Third Reich, as it tried to obliterate any trace of Jewish ancestry in a family that it held up as a perfect example of Aryanism. See chapter 22.

Emilie Sophia Anna Trampusch[14] was, by all accounts, an attractive and charming young woman who worked as a milliner. Ten years younger than Strauss, she lived in a small apartment in Kumpfgasse, close to St Stephen's Cathedral in the centre of the city. The Strausses' house was across the Danube canal in Taborstrasse, which ran alongside the leafy and green Augarten park, a carriage ride of not more than ten or fifteen minutes from St Stephen's.

It is probable the liaison began before Strauss left on that first tour. But what Anna was totally unprepared for was the news that reached her just two months after her youngest child, Eduard, was born. Emilie had borne Strauss an illegitimate daughter, and he was openly and brazenly admitting he was the father.

Far from being repentant, he continued the relationship, and exactly one year and ten days later Emilie gave birth again, this time to a son. He was christened Johann Wilhelm. Anna now had to contend not only with the fact that her husband had a second family, but that the eldest son was named Johann, just as her eldest son was.

It did not end there. Over the following ten years Emilie gave birth six more times. Only three of the eight children survived into adulthood and they were the three eldest, two daughters and a son. All three kept their mother's name, so that there was one Johann Strauss senior and two half-brothers, Johann Strauss junior and Johann Trampusch. None of the three illegitimate Strauss children has earned even a footnote in history. I find it surprising, given that

> *"There was no shortage of female admirers at his concerts, and Strauss was not reluctant to benefit from what was on offer."*

---

[14] Variously Trampusch, Trambusch, Tramposch. The name, in whichever form, is inelegant to Austrian ears and will have been mocked by her detractors.

Endlich wird der Wagen ganz zur Laterne.

Above

Caricature on the hysteria over Strauss and his unstoppable bandwagon.

their father was an extraordinarily gifted musician and their mother later became an actress – artistic talent therefore to some extent on both sides – that none of the three possessed any aptitude in music or any other of the arts.[15] It is perhaps even more surprising that his three legitimate sons all became prolific composers, one of undoubted genius.

Johann Strauss senior had fathered fourteen children with two women in twenty-one years. He had two families and ran two households, which was an open secret among musical circles in Vienna. During roughly the same period he had composed the best part of a hundred pieces, and his name was becoming known across Europe, which quite simply had never seen a musician like Johann Strauss.

---

[15] There is some evidence the eldest, Emilie, followed her mother onto the stage, but it is not known with what success.

He composed most of the pieces he performed. Broadly they were a mixture of gallops, waltzes and polkas, all designed for dance and amusement. They were not just trifles. It did not take the musically sophisticated Viennese long to realise these were substantial pieces, perfectly calculated to entertain an audience.

There was also his infectious personality. He did more than simply lead from the violin; the music seemed to inhabit his body. Swaying with the violin under his chin one moment, waving it – and the bow – in the air the next, turning to the audience while playing, smiling all the time. And his were not audiences sitting in serried rows of seats, formally attired, speaking only in the quietest of whispers, taking care not to cough. These were dance-hall audiences, eating, drinking, laughing, conversing and, most importantly of all, dancing.

Given his growing reputation it was hardly surprising when an invitation came to travel to the most sophisticated city, artistically speaking, in mainland Europe, where audiences were notoriously critical, even cruel. It would be a challenge, a risk. The Strauss sounds and rhythms might be much loved in central Europe, but how would they go down nearly eight hundred miles to the west, in Paris?

"He did more than simply lead from the violin; the music seemed to inhabit his body."

In the late afternoon of 4 October 1837 Johann Strauss and an orchestra of twenty-eight musicians boarded coaches for the overland journey to the French capital. There were several stop-offs on the way for concerts in southern Germany, and then in Strasbourg. They arrived in Paris on 27 October, no doubt exhausted from an arduous journey with performances along the way. The first concert was scheduled for 1 November, giving them just four days to recover, settle in and rehearse.

To add to his anxiety Strauss learned that tickets had been sold at inflated prices, and his nerves were hardly calmed when he was informed that the cream of Parisian musical society would be in the audience. The most recognisable, with his mop of carrot-coloured hair, was also the most revered, Hector Berlioz. Other respected names, if not at this first concert then at subsequent performances, were Meyerbeer, Cherubini, Auber and Adolphe Adam (whose most famous ballet *Giselle* was still four years off).

It was with understandable trepidation therefore that Johann Strauss mounted the podium in front of his orchestra in the Salle des Gymnases. He need not have worried. Using flattery once again as a potent weapon – '*Der Carneval in Paris*' and the '*Paris Walzer*' (which contained a quotation from *La Marseillaise* in waltz-time!) had been specially composed – even this sophisticated Parisian audience could not resist the infectious sounds and rhythms of the Strauss orchestra.

Berlioz himself, considered by many (including himself) to be the natural successor of Beethoven, no less, wrote in the *Journal des Débats*:

> *We knew the name of Strauss, but that was all. Of the fire, the intelligence, and the rhythmic feeling which his orchestra displays, we had no notion … Their waltzes are difficult to play, but how easily the Viennese accomplish it, how they charm us with their piquant rhythmic coquetry!*

Where Berlioz led others followed, and it can have come as no surprise to Strauss that he soon received a formal invitation to perform at the very top – at the Tuileries Palace in the presence of King Louis-Philippe of France.

This was a very different monarchy from the one that had been brutally terminated less than a half-century earlier. Louis-Philippe was a distant relative of the ill-fated Louis XVI and enjoyed a fully aristocratic upbringing, but had some sympathy with the revolutionaries' aims, if not methods, and was keen to portray himself as a man of the people. So successful was he, at least in the early years of his reign, that he earned the sobriquet 'The Bourgeois King'.

Strauss and his men walked along the same corridors that had been stormed and in which the blood of the Swiss Guard was spilled during the revolution, to be greeted personally by the king, which no doubt surprised Strauss who was more accustomed to the rigid etiquette and formality of Vienna. He was flattered to hear the king say, 'Your waltzes have been familiar to me for a long time, my dear Herr Strauss. It gives me all the more pleasure that you have done me the honour of appearing here personally.'

The success of the performance was a foregone conclusion. Afterwards Louis-Philippe made an impromptu speech of congratulations and thanks to the Viennese musicians, all enjoyed

champagne, and the king took both of Strauss's hands in his – all in all, a scenario that would have been unthinkable in the presence of a French monarch not many years before.

If the king represented the highest personage Strauss and his musicians were to meet during their stay in Paris, then unquestionably the single musical figure they were most honoured to meet was an Italian violinist whose name was known across Europe. Now in the autumn of his years, suffering from the syphilis he had contracted many years before and a recent bout of pneumonia, Niccolò Paganini attended one of Strauss's concerts incognito, slipping into the back row unseen.

But the disguise was instantly spotted and he was ushered to the front of the hall and into a place of honour. Strauss came onto the podium, had his attention directed to the famous musician, instantly left the podium and the two men embraced. In a faltering voice, but clear enough for the audience to hear, Paganini said, 'I am glad to meet a man who has brought so much joy to the world.'

Everywhere the orchestra went they were lauded and applauded. Strauss's musicians were aware that they belonged to the most in-demand orchestra in Europe, that they were travelling to towns and cities they could not otherwise have expected to see in a normal lifetime, meeting royalty, aristocrats, composers, fellow musicians. Yet for the first time since Strauss formed his orchestra, there were the beginnings of an undercurrent of malaise. Not too strong, at least not to begin with, but a matter he would sooner or later have to confront.

By February 1838 the musicians had been away from home and family for the best part of five months, including over Christmas. Several of them had written home bemoaning the fact that the French did not take much notice of Christmas – no Christmas trees! – and when they did it was without a proper sense of its religious significance: dancing in the streets when they should have been attending midnight Mass.

There was a growing feeling among the players that it was time to return to Vienna. Strauss was aware of the demands he was making on them, the exhausting journeys by horse-drawn carriage, the busy schedule of concerts – often arranged at the last minute. One player wrote home that they were all enjoying a midday meal nine days before Christmas, when Strauss rushed in and told them to hurry up because they needed to leave for Rouen where they had just been booked to play at a masked ball and give three more concerts.

To head off any complaints about conditions, Strauss had made it a policy to spare no expense when it came to comfort. For the four months of the stay in Paris he took over an entire hotel, and in the particularly harsh Paris winter of 1836–7 he ordered every room to be individually heated. Meals were frequent and abundant, consisting of several courses. All players were paid promptly, and one wrote that several of the men, himself included, had received salary in advance when required. 'Strauss cares for his men just as a fond father cares for his children,' he put it.

But still there were rumblings of discontent, and Strauss knew what no one else in the party knew. There had been a development that was bound to bring matters to a head.

Niccolò Paganini.

Across the Channel the people of Britain were preparing for what they knew to be imminent: the death of the old king and the accession to the throne of a young princess by the name of Victoria. The coronation would unleash festivities such as the country had not seen for a long time, and the invitation had come to Johann Strauss for his orchestra to be part of it. Not only had he a pocketful of invitations to perform for members of the aristocracy, but he could also expect to play in the presence of the princess, soon to be queen, in Buckingham Palace. This would be the pinnacle for the young Viennese musician and his orchestra. Turning it down was simply not an option.

Strauss's reputation had travelled ahead of him and already there was excitement that this new dance, the waltz, might soon be coming to British shores, with all the opportunities it offered for romance, illicit liaisons and sexual intrigue – none of these pursuits entirely unknown in British aristocratic circles. Sophisticated appetites had been whetted by no less a figure than the poet Lord Byron, who had written:

Gods! how the glorious theme my strain exalts
And rhyme finds partner rhyme in praise of 'Waltz' …
Round all the confines of the yielded waist
The strangest hand may wander undisplaced;
The lady's in return may grasp as much
As princely paunches may offer to her touch …
Thus front to front the partners move or stand,
The foot may rest, but none withdraw the hand …
The breast thus publicly resign'd to man,
In private may resist him – if it can.

Strauss delayed announcing to his orchestra until towards the end of the stay in Paris that they were soon to leave for London. His logic was that he wanted nothing to upset the remaining concerts. On the other hand, as the final concert approached there was a palpable feeling of release among the men; soon they would be returning home to Vienna. Predictably the simmering tension broke through to the surface when Strauss made his plans known. One particularly troublesome member of the orchestra, who led a small breakaway faction, convinced his supporters that if they once set foot on board a ship they would be parted from Europe for ever. He, and they, refused point-blank to follow Strauss.

Strauss took a two-pronged approach to the revolt. First he used attack as a means of defence, reminding the men they had all signed contracts, which he could hold them to. Secondly he stressed how he appreciated all the hard work they had done, how he admired their obvious devotion to him, and how he could guarantee them a pay increase based on the firm offers of work in England. Finally he said that after a lot of thought if any of them absolutely refused to travel further, he would release them from their contract and allow them to return home.

Four members of the orchestra left. It was thus a barely depleted party of musicians, Johann Strauss at their head, who boarded the appropriately named steamship *Princess Victoria* in the Dutch port of Flushing on the night of 11 April 1838 for the crossing to England, and the orchestra's biggest adventure yet.

Chapter Four

BY ROYAL APPOINTMENT

I **have used the word** 'gruelling' to describe the schedule for Johann Strauss I and his orchestra in previous months. Now they were about to learn what that word really meant. Over the following nine months they would perform well over a hundred times, averaging around four concerts a week, constantly journeying throughout England north and south, as well as making trips to Scotland and Ireland. Strauss continued to compose, as well as directing the orchestra, responding to invitations, arranging travel, booking accommodation, and generally managing the lives – all the tensions, rivalries, minor disputes, unscheduled absences, occasional over-indulgence in alcohol, homesickness – of an orchestra on the road.

Small wonder the itinerary would end in total physical breakdown for Strauss, with London's leading musical journal, *The Musical World*, reporting (with a touch of malice): 'Strauss, who is on his hotel bed, finds himself successful, much applauded, very rich – and dying.'

It began badly. After a difficult overnight Channel crossing, Strauss found that the hotel he had booked in London's Leicester Square not only could not accommodate the entire party, causing some of the men to stay elsewhere, but it was also not clean, did not have a dining room, and the food was poor. To exacerbate matters Strauss discovered soon after checking in that a large sum of money, almost £100, had been stolen from his room.

There was nothing he could do immediately, since the first concert was scheduled in less than a week at the Queen's Concert Rooms in Hanover Square. His priority was arranging the programme and rehearsing. Strauss's mood was hardly improved when

he learned that tickets were not selling well – poor weather, lack of advertising, a hit on at Covent Garden, and ridiculously expensive tickets at 10/6d.[16]

It is not hard to imagine the weariness with which Strauss must have mounted the podium, and the feeling of 'here we go again' among the players. That might account for the review in the following morning's *Times*, which accused Strauss of so drilling conformity

---

[16] A comparison with today's prices is difficult, but a rough equivalent would be between £80 and £100.

Right

A plaque marks the hotel where Strauss first stayed in Leicester Square.

and precision into his orchestra, that 'an effect is produced like that of an accurately constructed machine'.

Soon afterwards Strauss, known for his fieriness and quick temper, exploded. Things had got on top of him and the tour had barely started. He ordered his men to leave the awful hotel immediately, without giving due notice. The hotel proprietor, a certain George Street, took Strauss to court, and so Europe's most famous travelling composer and orchestral leader found himself up before a bewigged judge in London, in a scene that might well have inspired a young London author by the name of Charles Dickens.

Strauss was fortunate to escape with a fine of just £27 16s, but was ordered to pay court costs of £140, money that he did not have. Under Britain's notorious bankruptcy laws debtor prison beckoned for the whole entourage, which would have brought the nascent tour to an embarrassing and undignified end. The perilous situation was saved by a London music publisher named Robert Cocks, who offered to put the money up in return for the rights to publish Strauss's waltzes in Britain. Strauss knew this would cause problems with his Austrian publisher Tobias Haslinger, but reasoned that he had more chance of squaring things back in Vienna than in a strange city whose customs and laws were alien to him, whose people he did not know, and whose language he did not speak.

He therefore accepted Mr Cocks' offer, something for which the London publisher had reason to be grateful many times over in the coming years. The court case was resolved and the tour was back on.

⟶∞⟵

Between that first concert on 17 April and the end of July, Strauss and his orchestra gave a total of seventy-nine performances in London alone, and the list of hosts for whom he performed reads like a *Who's Who* of English aristocracy: the Duke of Wellington, the Duke of Devonshire, the Duke of Cambridge, the Duke of Buccleuch and Sutherland, the Countess of Cadogan and Mrs Lionel de Rothschild, as well as the ambassadors of Austria and France. There were also two public balls, two charity concerts, thirty-nine public concerts, and three large-scale concerts shared with other high-profile artists.[17]

The ultimate accolade, though, came with the invitation to perform in the presence of the young Princess Victoria in Buckingham House, the building she was about to make her official royal palace. This took place on 10 May, and Strauss followed his usual practice of performing a piece specially composed for the occasion. This was the waltz *'Hommage à la Reine d'Angleterre'*,[18] which tactfully quoted from *'Rule, Britannia'* in its introduction and *'God Save the Queen'* in waltz tempo in its coda. *The Times* reported that Strauss's new waltz was much admired by the future queen, and thereafter Strauss made sure he included it in future performances following the coronation, both at the Palace and elsewhere on tour.

And what a tour he now embarked on. Even while resident in London, Strauss and the orchestra made a five-day visit to Cheltenham and Bath, and on leaving London at the end of July they began a

---

[17] At the ball given by the Duke of Sutherland, Strauss was also a guest, invited to join the Duke's table after the performance, a practice not uncommon in Paris or Vienna, but practically unheard of in the class-conscious milieu of Britain.

[18] Although the coronation of Queen Victoria was still six weeks away.

Above

Buckingham House, which, as Buckingham Palace, the young Queen Victoria made the official residence of the British monarchy.

six-week tour of England, Scotland and Ireland. In all they would perform in thirty-one different towns and cities, making return visits by popular demand to several of them.

On many days they gave three performances in three different venues: matinee, late afternoon, and evening. It was reported Strauss could now command fees of £200 or more for a performance – a substantial amount at that time. The constant travel was made easier by advances in modes of transport. Strauss himself wrote of the tour:

> *I found myself in a different town almost daily, as one may travel here exceedingly quickly by virtue of the good horses and excellent roads … Of great advantage to the traveller are the railways, which I have used extensively, in Liverpool, Manchester, Birmingham, etc. …*

But there was one feature of life in the United Kingdom over which Strauss could have no control: the weather. October in Scotland was cold and wet. There was a week of ceaseless rain, coaches had trouble making headway through the mud, and several members of the orchestra came down with colds or worse. A local doctor prescribed a concoction of claret, nutmeg and ginger, 'hot enough to wake the dead'. Still they performed. It was thus a group of musicians of depleted strength that made the crossing to Ireland, and all the more so on their return.

It was inevitable that sooner or later a work schedule of this intensity would catch up with Strauss and his men. It did so in the north of England. In November Strauss was reported to be suffering from 'illness of a serious character'. He had severe shivering fits, a hacking cough and chest pains. Concerts in Derby and Leicester were postponed. A doctor in Derby did little to improve things, by prescribing Strauss a dangerously strong dose of opium that almost killed him.

It is possible, even probable, that Strauss did not receive much sympathy from his men. This time they really had had enough. They had been away from home now for over a year, and they wanted to return to Vienna. A small but militant clique warned Strauss that if he did not promise that they would leave for home soon, they would refuse to play on.

There was another factor at work here, hidden not so far beneath the surface. The members of the orchestra were well aware of Johann Strauss's domestic arrangements back home in Vienna. He had a wife and children in the family home on the edge of the Augarten. He also had a mistress and illegitimate children in the apartment he had set up for them near St Stephen's Cathedral in the centre of the city.

Life for Strauss in Vienna was complicated. Life on tour, on the road, was an escape from all that. What if it was his plan, they conjectured, never to return? To stay away on tour for year after year. And how could he achieve that? Simple. By putting into action a plan he had mentioned more than once: the ultimate ambition. Board a ship for the United States. Succeed there, and there would be no need ever to return to Vienna and all the complications it held for him. Had he not implied as much when they were on tour in Ireland? Look west, he had told them, there is nothing between here and America. That is where we *must* go.

As a new decade dawned, so did a new feeling that the repression of the last twenty or more years could not endure. Whispers became voices. The cosy domesticity of the Biedermeier era contained within itself the inevitable seeds of change. We know now, with the benefit of hindsight, that it would be just a few more years before change would come, and that when it did it would explode with a force that would change Europe for ever.

What Johann Strauss could not in his most fantastical dreams have imagined was that when change did come, it would not only sweep away the established order, it would take him along with it.

Chapter Five
A FAMILY CONSPIRACY

*I*t was not just a different Vienna that Johann Strauss returned to, but a subtly altered set – or sets – of domestic circumstances. It appears Strauss did not just prefer the company of his mistress and illegitimate family, but had developed an intense disregard for his wife and legitimate children.

While he was abroad on tour he had used an intermediary to send large amounts of money – secretly – to Emilie Trampusch. On his return he moved back into the large family house, the Hirschenhaus, but lived in a separate apartment within it. Whether he insisted on this arrangement, or Anna banished him to his own quarters, is not known. Quite probably it was Johann's doing, since the apartment gave him room to live and work: he could compose there, he had an office from which to run the orchestra's complicated schedule, and in the large main room there was space actually to rehearse with his players. Anna would also have been forced to rely on him for housekeeping money. He held the purse strings, literally.

His wife's public humiliation was made complete by the fact that in the seven years after his return to Vienna he fathered a further five children with Emilie. He might have lived in the family house but he clearly spent a lot of time in the Kumpfgasse. The atmosphere in the Hirschenhaus, at least when Strauss was there, must have been tense, to say the least. He was not happy in the company of his family, and the clear dislike he had for his wife was something he also exhibited towards his children.

The two elder boys were developing a talent for playing the piano, and Johann II would recall in later years how he and Josef would watch their father conduct orchestral rehearsals in the house, 'paying close attention to every note, so that we familiarised ourselves with his style and then played what we heard straight off, in exactly the same spirited manner as he had. He was our ideal.'

The admiration was not reciprocated. Johann said his father had no idea his two sons were talented pianists and that when they finally demonstrated their skills to him, he accused them of 'tinkling at the keys in an amateurish fashion'.

Their father went further. There was to be no thought on either of their parts of a career in music. He would not allow it. Instead they were to continue with normal school studies. And so in 1841, when Johann was fifteen and Josef thirteen, they were enrolled as students in the Commercial Studies Department of the Polytechnic Institute of Vienna. Strauss planned a career in banking for his eldest son, and engineering for the younger.

Johann II, at least, had other plans, and he confided in his closest ally, his mother. He was in no doubt that he wanted his future to be in music. Furthermore he had no intention of becoming a banker, nor did he intend remaining at the Polytechnic Institute. His mother, it appears, sided entirely with him, and it is not difficult to understand why. In the first place Johann's musical talent was blindingly obvious, and his father's refusal to see it must have been deliberate obstinacy. The boy had actually composed his first waltz at the age of six and given the manuscript page with a mere twenty-one bars of a simple melody in three-four time to an impressed mother.

Now, at the same time as attending the Polytechnic Institute and with money in the household in short supply, he was giving music lessons to children of friends. He was himself just fifteen years of age, and he was already bringing in funds with his natural talent at the piano.

Probably too there was the feeling at the back of Anna's mind that to do something surreptitious, that her husband was unaware of, would be somehow getting back at him for the hurt he had caused her. And what if her eldest son proved to have real musical talent? Wouldn't that be a delicious irony? What better way for her and her family to avenge themselves than by outstripping her husband in the very area in which he excelled?

So when Johann came to his mother and said he wanted to give up his studies and devote himself to music, he found a willing and accommodating pair of ears. There was more to Johann's plan. He did not want simply to become a musician so that he could perform at the piano, or earn a living giving piano lessons. Oh no, his mind was set on greater things. He had observed his father and learned from him. He admired what his father was doing in music. He might not have enjoyed anything approaching a close father–son relationship, but his father – unwittingly – was providing him with knowledge and inspiration, and his son, even at the tender age of fifteen, knew exactly what use he intended to make of this.

He turned to his mother. He wanted to learn the violin. He knew his father would never agree to this. He wanted to reach a level of proficiency where he could form his own orchestra and give concerts of his own compositions. In other words, to follow exactly in his father's musical footsteps. He assured his mother that he could pay for lessons with the money his own teaching was bringing in. Anna willingly entered the conspiracy and went straight into the enemy camp, as it were, by approaching one Franz Amon, first violinist in her husband's own orchestra, who deputised for him on occasion as conductor with a second group when Strauss himself was on tour.

Clearly Anna knew Amon well enough to know that he would not divulge the plan to her husband. She was right. Amon agreed to teach the young Johann, and to keep it secret from his employer. Discretion was obviously paramount but an indication of just how little interest Strauss took in his children is evidenced by the fact that Johann left the Polytechnic Institute within a year to take lessons from Amon and devote himself full time to music, and his father had no idea.

Above

Johann Strauss's long-suffering wife, Anna Streim, matriarch of the Strauss dynasty.

It was a fairly remarkable act of faith on the part of Franz Amon. He was presumably risking his job in teaching a teenager who seemed to have a precocious musical talent, but can hardly have yet shown signs of the compositional genius he would later display. It is possible Amon had some grudge against Strauss senior, or even that he disapproved of Strauss's treatment of his family.

Whatever lay behind it, Amon not only began giving Johann secret lessons, he also tutored him in exactly the skills of his father – not simply to play the violin, but to stand up and sway in time to

Right
Johann Strauss the
Younger's violin,
which survived
into the twentieth
century, but was
destroyed when the
Nazis sacked Vienna.

the music, in effect to lead from the violin. He also taught him to perform the three-four rhythm of the waltz, to create a yearning and languid phrase, to slow down towards the middle, to give just a moment's hiatus at the high point of the melody before continuing – all details that would later instantly identify a piece as being by Johann Strauss the Younger.

Amon was, of course, able to do this only because of Johann's innate and extraordinary musical talent, which the older man quickly recognised. He soon realised, too, that there would come a point when he no longer had anything to teach Johann, particularly in the field of composition, and so after a while he passed Johann on first to an organist who was an experienced composer, and then to a professional violin teacher who played at the Vienna Court Opera.

Johann Strauss II was becoming a seriously good violinist, with a natural talent for composition, and in a city such as Vienna this could not stay secret for long. Sooner or later word was bound to reach his father, and reach him it did. Johann recalled later in life that one fine day he was playing the violin in front of a mirror in his room, swaying as he played, ascertaining which particular bodily movements were more elegant than others, when the door opened and his father walked in.

'What?' Johann recalled his father shouting. 'You play the violin?' Johann said his father had heard on the musical grapevine that he had ambitions to become a professional musician, but regarded it as a ridiculous idea since he had no idea in the first place that his son even played the violin. According to the son there was 'a violent and unpleasant scene'. He apparently tried to reason with his father, to interest him in his aims, but his father 'wanted to know nothing of my plans'.

One can imagine the hurt this must have caused the teenage boy. Every boy hoping to follow in his father's footsteps wants to make him proud, and the total rejection must have seriously wounded him. It is true that Johann was recalling the incident many years after it happened, but the actions that Strauss would go on to take suggest that Johann was not exaggerating. In fact it is hard to believe that a father could be as callous, uncaring and vindictive as Strauss was about to show himself to be.

Strauss senior spared barely a thought for his precociously talented eldest son. He had no need to. He had never been as busy or as popular. In the first half of the new decade he made guest appearances with his orchestra in Austria, Hungary, Austrian Silesia, Saxony, Prussia and Germany, as well as fulfilling numerous engagements in Vienna.

In 1843 his former friend and rival Joseph Lanner, the only other musician who had ever come anywhere close to challenging him, died of typhus infection two days after his forty-second birthday. Johann Strauss now stood alone as composer and orchestra leader, the undisputed master of his genre in the city of music. To cement this unrivalled reputation, he was about to earn the title 'Waltz

"*From the moment he put together an orchestra, Strauss the Younger left no one in any doubt as to who was in charge.*"

King' with the most masterly waltz he had composed to date, the '*Lorelei-Rhein-Klänge*' ('Echoes of the Rhine Lorelei'). The opening phrase, crowned with a *fortissimo* chord, then repeated, immediately secured the audience's attention, before the waltz launched into a melody so beguiling it was soon being whistled and hummed on the streets of Vienna.

Vienna had its Waltz King. It was Johann Strauss the Elder. Nothing and no one could displace him.

No one except his namesake: his eldest son. Johann II was about to launch a challenge, one that could, potentially, hardly be more devastating or humiliating. But a challenge was all it was. Strauss had nothing to fear. His son had a modicum of talent, nothing more. He most certainly did not have either the talent or the resources to see his challenge become reality.

And what was this challenge? Strauss could hardly believe it when he heard about it. On 3 August 1844, a year and two months short of his twentieth birthday, Johann Strauss the Younger, armed with excellent testimonials from his two highly respected teachers, approached the Viennese authorities with an extraordinary request:

> *I intend to play with an orchestra of twelve to fifteen players in res-taurants, specifically at Dommayer's in Hietzing, whose manager has already assured me that I can hold musical entertainments there as soon as my orchestra is in order. I have not yet determined the remaining venues, but I believe I will be able to secure sufficient engagements and income …*

Johann was being nothing if not bold. As yet he had no orchestra worthy of the name. He did the rounds of taverns where itinerant musicians played, particularly the Zur Stadt Belgrad ('At the City of Belgrade'), which was well known for its musical entertainment. He hired musicians, trained them, dismissed some, kept others, engaged more.

On 5 September Johann junior was probably as surprised as anyone when the municipal council granted his request. He now showed himself to be his father's son. A month later, calling himself 'Herr Kapellmeister Johann Strauss',[19] he drew up a carefully

---

[19] Not easily translatable. The closest might be 'Concert Master and Conductor', or 'Music Director'. At any rate, the most senior musician.

Above

A hand-coloured lantern
slide of Dommayer's
Casino (c. 1910), the
suburban tavern where
Johann Strauss the
Younger was to give
his first concert in
October 1844.

worded one-year contract with twenty-four musicians, detailing the rights and obligations of the parties under eight separate sections, including rules on punctuality and discipline at rehearsals and performances, as well as details of how issues such as illness, prohibition of substitutes, settlement of disputes, even the careful handling of musical instruments, should be dealt with.

From the very moment he put together an orchestra, Johann Strauss the Younger left no one in any doubt as to who was in charge. It was his orchestra, not just in substance, but in name too, and woe betide any musician who thought otherwise.

There were now two Johann Strauss orchestras in Vienna. One was thoroughly professional, with many tours behind it, garlanded wherever it went. The other was a motley bunch of ill-trained musicians with little or no experience, who had never played together before, certainly not in an orchestra of this size, with no understanding of the discipline and cooperation it would require.

Furthermore, while Strauss senior could command the most prestigious dance halls in Vienna, it appeared his son had secured a tavern in the suburb of Hietzing, opposite the Schönbrunn park, with the unsophisticated name of Dommayer's Casino. It was practically out of town. No one who really mattered would bother to make the journey. The audience would be regulars enjoying a drink and a chat.

Johann Strauss senior was confident he had nothing to fear from his precocious and overly ambitious son. Just as well, because his attention was diverted in another direction. Anna Strauss, fed up with her husband's misbehaviour and emboldened by her son's extraordinary courage and willpower, sued for divorce.

Chapter Six
'GOOD MORNING
STRAUSS SON!'

There was a lot of ill will, venom even, flying around over Johann the Younger's proposed debut concert, and it was entirely in one direction – from father to son. Legends have abounded from that day to this of the measures Strauss took to prevent his son's concert from even taking place.

It was said he sent a loyal colleague around all the main dance halls to tell the manager that if Johann was allowed to stage his concert there, he – the famous Strauss – would never perform there again. It is more than likely something of the sort took place since, although Dommayer's was hardly a prime venue, Strauss, who had played there many times in the past, was never to do so again.

Tickets for the concert were selling extremely well, despite the relative difficulty of getting to the venue. Strauss senior, stunned by this news, came to the conclusion his son was achieving this by sheer fraud. The posters advertising the concert had the name JOHANN STRAUSS in large capital letters in bold print, with the word *Sohn* ['Son'] in small letters, not bold, in brackets underneath. Strauss and his supporters accused Johann of deliberately trying to pass himself off as his father, to ensure a good audience.

Unable to prevent the concert from taking place despite his claims, Strauss senior announced that he would give a concert on the same evening. In the end this did not materialise, possibly because ticket sales had gone so well that he feared his own concert might be less well attended than his son's.

The most persistent legend is that Strauss, with the help of that same loyal colleague, organised a 'claque', a group of supporters to attend the younger Johann's concert and disrupt it. This seems an unnaturally harsh course of action for a father to take against presume he would follow in his father's footsteps. If his compositions were not up to the mark, well, there was time for improvement, but he would probably be unlikely to progress beyond being a band leader. Good composers started young.

There might well have been a small gasp of recognition as Johann walked self-consciously out onto the stage. The same hair, jet black and curly, as his famous father, dark gleaming eyes, and a similar swagger of self-confidence, even if it masked an inner nervousness. The clothes, too, no less flamboyant than his father's – blue tailcoat with silver buttons, embroidered silk waistcoat, grey trousers looped under buckled shoes – even if they were, as rumour had it, borrowed for the night.

The similarity went much further, as one reviewer remarked in print the following day. Not just a similar facial expression, but the way he held and played his violin, the bow grasped with the tips of the fingers, graceful gestures of the lower part of the arm, swift energetic bowing. And, in the most noticeable influence of his father, a sudden turning to the audience, spraying sparks from his violin 'as if from a galvanic battery'. This was the son, proving as adept and mesmerising a performer as his father. So far.

A polite, respectful reception for works by other composers. But Johann braced himself for what he knew was the most important moment of his nascent musical career. He had scheduled a waltz of his own. Originally entitled *'Das Mutterherz'* ('The Heart of a Mother') in tribute to the one person who had made it possible for him to pursue his dream, the sensible and down-to-earth Anna had persuaded him to alter it. He chose *'Die Gunstwerber'* ('Seekers of Favour').

Johann raised the violin and settled it comfortably under his chin. The whole top part of his body bent into the opening triplet of chords, played *fortissimo*. The audience could not but pay attention. The chords repeated, leading into a gentle lyrical passage which itself led into as beguiling a waltz as this audience had heard, instantly as charming as anything his father had written. Turning at the *crescendo* to face the audience, forcing them to sway with him, he looked back to the orchestra, before turning again and playing a beautiful, melodious solo passage on the violin, gazing out at the audience and smiling as he did so.

They were mesmerised. Another waltz theme, before returning to the first that had followed the opening chords, this time met with

a smile of recognition by the audience. Solo violin again, played as if for each individual member of the audience, leading to a final quickened flourish calculated to bring on applause.

Which it most certainly did. Applause and more applause. An encore, and another, and another. Johann had to repeat *'Die Gunstwerber'* no fewer than four times. After that he could do no wrong. More pieces by established composers, then another waltz of his own, *'Die Sinngedichte'* ('Poems of the Senses'). Contemporary reports said this piece had to be repeated *nineteen* times. Whether an exaggeration or not, the message was clear. Johann junior had triumphed.

But the single most moving moment of the whole evening came quite unexpectedly, catching the audience unaware. It was a calculated gesture on Johann's part, which he had rehearsed with his orchestra. It needed no introduction. There must have

Open discontent first seeped out onto the streets in Paris and other French cities, and workers and students in other countries were quick to follow suit. Vienna, in particular, was about to catch fire and Metternich would feel the full force of popular fury.

Given the power and speed with which revolutionary fervour swept Europe, it is perhaps surprising that it produced few lasting effects. The uprisings were ultimately nothing more sophisticated than an attempt at mob rule; long on enthusiasm and very short indeed on organisation.

Vienna though was something of an exception. True, the revolution was brutally put down, but not before Metternich and his wife fled the city under cover of darkness. Before the year was out there would be a new emperor on the Habsburg throne, a much younger man than before and one who was more likely to respond to the discontent.

This was a monumental change at the time, albeit less perceptible a few years on. What was entirely new, though, was an attitude, an empowerment. The working classes, who had never been heard before, now had a voice, even if it was somewhat muted.

It was the beginning of a new era – in music as well as in so much else. Vienna had a new emperor, and a new Waltz King.

Chapter Seven

RADETZKY MARCHES OUT OF STEP

*I*t began with a relatively insignificant incident. It was an act of violence, resulting in unnecessary deaths, but it could have been contained. As had happened before and would happen again, this was the spark that lit a tinderbox of anger and discontent.

At one o'clock on Monday, 13 March 1848, a small detachment of soldiers fired a volley of shots into a motley crowd of students, workers and general malcontents who had forced their way past heavy gates into the courtyard outside the Lower Austrian Landhaus. Their orders had been to fire warning shots above the heads of the demonstrators, but they panicked and fired directly into the crowd.

At least five fell dead and many more were wounded. What could have remained a little local trouble rapidly escalated. Angry demonstrators broke into the city armoury. Outside the city gates, which had been closed, government buildings were smashed, machinery destroyed, and factories set on fire.

By the end of the day several dozen people had been killed. It was enough to precipitate a series of events that would change Vienna and Austria for ever. The demands of the demonstrators were the culmination of more than thirty years of repression. In themselves they were not particularly extreme: freedom of the press, public accounting of government expenditure, an end to constantly rising food prices, more representation for the middle classes in government.

But they were, in effect, a declaration of war against the rule of law, and the chancellor who had single-handedly and ruthlessly imposed it for the past several decades: Klemens von Metternich.

Beyond their domestic demands, there was something else on the malcontents' agenda: an end to Austrian rule in northern Italy. Unlikely though it might seem, this demand would have a direct impact on the lives of the city's most famous musical dynasty, dividing the Strauss family down the middle, older generation against younger, in a way from which it would never recover.

As part of the Austrian empire's expansionist policy, its army was in occupation of northern Italy. With Vienna in disarray the order soon went south to the commander of the Austrian army not to engage the Italian nationalist forces but to maintain a ceasefire. The commander ignored the order and engaged the Italians at Custozza, where he scored a decisive victory on 24 and 25 July.

Milan and Lombardy were preserved for the empire, to the joy of the old guard in Vienna. But while the governing class and the military celebrated, the revolutionaries vented their disgust. What right did Austria have to occupy any territory beyond its borders? Their anger increased when the Austrian army went on to further victories, shoring up Austrian rule across northern Italy.

Such was the joy, though, in the mansions and stately homes of the Establishment that the decision was made to honour the Austrian commander and his army with a 'Grand Impressive Victory Festival' to be held on the Wasserglacis, the wide expanse of green outside the city wall.

Johann Strauss senior was commissioned to compose a new piece in honour of the Austrian commander, which he gladly accepted. What better way to establish his pre-eminent position above all fellow composers in Vienna, including his own son?

The celebrations were planned for 31 August, and so time was short. Strauss took two Viennese folk songs, reworked them, and composed a new piece in the form of a march. Legend has it that it took him just two hours to compose the piece, which given how prodigious he was might well be true, or at least not too much of an exaggeration.

Strauss named the piece, naturally, for the man in whose honour he had written it. That was the eighty-two-year-old commander-in-chief of the Austrian army, Field-Marshal Johann Josef Wenzel, Count Radetzky von Radetz.

Strauss could not have known it at the time, but that swiftly written little piece would ensure his immortality. The instantly catchy tune, the bouncing rhythm; it is practically impossible not to tap one's fingers, or stamp one's feet, in time to the music. In fact it is traditional – not just in Vienna, but across the globe – to clap in time to the music. It is, of course, the world-famous *'Radetzky March'*.

Johann Josef Wenzel, Count Radetzky von Radetz, a name immortalised in the most famous piece of music composed by Johann Strauss the Elder.

The two Johann Strausses, father and son, were divided emotionally and professionally. The son resented the father for walking out and shamelessly starting a second family. Now each was running his own orchestra, competing for dates in the same venues. To make matters worse, when workers and students took to the streets of Vienna in the revolution of 1848, father and son took opposing sides. Strauss senior, now in middle age, instinctively supported the old regime, the established order. His *'Radetzky March'* commission cemented this.

Johann, his son, saw things very differently, on several occasions actually helping to man the barricades. Like most young men of his age he wanted change, and change was what was happening. Within days of the fatal shootings on 13 March, the unthinkable happened.

Chancellor Metternich, who had until this point been able to rely on the total support of the Habsburg monarchy, now found that support haemorrhaging away. The ineffectual emperor, beset with ill health, allowed others around him to wield power, and they needed a scapegoat. They found it in the man who had governed so ruthlessly for decades but now found that events were slipping from his control. The chancellor must resign, they declared. And not just resign, but flee the city and the country. The Metternich era was over.[21]

Johann made no secret of his sympathies for the revolutionaries, among whom he had many friends. In May he became kapellmeister of the National Guard, which sided with the students, and composed a string of numbers with titles such as *'Revolutions-Marsch'*

---

[21] Metternich and his wife settled first in London and then Brighton. He was regularly visited by the Duke of Wellington and Benjamin Disraeli, both of whom he briefed on European affairs. He openly resented not being contacted for advice by his successors in Vienna, and is said never once to have admitted any faults in his long career.

('Revolution March'), *'Barrikaden-Lieder'* ('Songs of the Barricades'), which he retitled *'Freiheits-Lieder'* ('Songs of Freedom'), and *'Burschen-Lieder'* ('Students' Songs').

Both Johann and Josef spent at least some time helping man the barricades, and Johann found himself briefly under arrest in December for playing *'La Marseillaise'* in public, a clear sign of support for fellow revolutionaries in Paris. In his defence he stated that there was no political or nationalistic motive behind any piece he chose to play; in fact he had done his best to avoid controversy. Somewhat disingenuously he blamed the demands of the audience, who he feared might riot if he did not satisfy their demands. The case against him was dropped.

On 2 December 1848, in case anyone doubted that change was truly happening, the feeble emperor abdicated, and his nephew Franz Josef became Emperor of Austria. The old guard resented the change, pointing to the fact that Franz Josef was a mere eighteen years of age, trained for the military not government, and would be deposed, or forced to abdicate, within a short while.

In fact Franz Josef – 'Franzl' – would reign for almost sixty-eight years, almost the longest-ruling monarch in European history. He would live into the First World War, and preside over the downfall of the House of Habsburg. In his lifetime he would have to endure more personal tragedy than any man or woman should ever have to know.

His long life would also, at several points, intersect with that of the musician whose compositions would define his reign, the man who, in a single piece of music around ten minutes long, would provide a greater insight into the character of Franz Josef than many hundreds of pages of biography.

But that still lay in the future. Now, as the mid-point in the turbulent nineteenth century approached, a truly new era in Vienna was dawning. The Viennese knew it; so did their new emperor. Young Johann Strauss and his brothers were in no doubt. The same could not entirely be said of their father.

Johann Strauss senior took his orchestra back on tour, and an extensive tour it was. He needed to get out of Vienna. In the wake of the demonstrations and violence the people were restless. The annual new-year carnival, the *Fasching*, was a lacklustre affair in 1849. The populace wanted more than concerts to appease them. And, whether he liked it or not, Strauss was associated with the old regime, the past that had gone for ever. Was he not, after all, the composer of the *'Radetzky March'*?

He took his orchestra first to Prague, and was stunned when protesters gathered outside his hotel chanting revolutionary slogans. He had never been the target of political demonstrations before. He was, simply, a musician.

At the performance the night following his arrival, he made a decision that went against every artistic fibre in his body. He was acting on advice, though he could scarcely believe he was following it. For the sake of public order, he dropped the *'Radetzky March'* from the programme. And still there were boos interlaced with the cheers.

After a brief return to Vienna, he left with the orchestra – thirty-two strong – for Germany. There, at least, he could be sure of a warm welcome, if past experience was anything to go by. But nothing was the same: the glory days were over.

Ulm and Munich in Bavaria, traditional, Catholic areas, close to Austria, were warm towards him, but as he travelled west and north, the hostility grew. Augsburg, Stuttgart, Heidelberg, Heilbronn, Mannheim, Mainz, Koblenz, Bonn, Cologne, Aachen. To some degree or other, it seemed, no matter where he went, he encountered hostility.

Even though he had dropped the *'Radetzky March'* from the programme, even distributing cockades in the republican colours of black, red and gold for his men to pin to their Old German hats. But it made no difference. He was a black-and-yellow, whether he liked it or not – the colours of the Habsburg monarchy. The old days of adoring crowds were gone.

Nowhere was it worse than in Frankfurt. The audience shouted 'Berlioz! Berlioz!' and demanded the *'Rakoczy March'*, which Berlioz had written in honour of the leader of the popular uprising a century earlier against Habsburg rule in Hungary. The irony of the similarity in names of the two pieces cannot have been lost on Strauss. In the event he played neither. Nor can he have failed to remember the rapturous reception the same Berlioz had given to his music in Paris ten years earlier.

A deep depression settled over Johann Strauss I. His music was being rejected. *He* was being rejected. There were domestic problems at home in Vienna, political issues on tour, and his finances were anything but secure. He wrote to music publishers, booksellers and music agents in advance of arrival to ask them to arrange

> *"A deep depression settled over Johann Strauss. His music was being rejected. He was being rejected."*

accommodation, concert venues and publicity. He told them in letters that he could not afford to stay in any particular town without a guaranteed number of performances.

He was pleased to get out of Germany and head down the Rhine into Belgium, where the reception in Brussels, Antwerp and Ostend was more along the lines he was used to. The farther he travelled from home, the less his association with the old regime mattered.

There was one destination where he could be sure of a truly warm welcome, where his political affiliations, if anything, would count in his favour. Eleven years earlier he and his orchestra had been lauded and lionised, and he knew he could count on the same again. On the night of 21 April 1849, he and his orchestra crossed the Channel to England.

He need not have worried about securing enough engagements. London, Reading, Oxford, Cheltenham, with many repeat visits. In a stay of two and a half months the Strauss Orchestra gave a total of forty-six performances, not far short of five concerts a week for ten weeks. A truly gruelling schedule.

The highlight, as before, was a performance at Buckingham Palace in the presence of Queen Victoria and Prince Albert. This was at a state ball before 1,600 guests, and for the occasion Strauss had composed his *Alice-Polka'* in honour of the queen's six-year-old daughter.

Other new compositions were performed at other venues, and at Exeter Hall in London Strauss shared the stage with a Viennese singer making her first visit to England. She was described in a London newspaper as 'a handsome woman, with a ripe mezzo-soprano voice, a charming style, and great dramatic feeling'.

The singer was Jetty Treffz, though that was not her real name, and she will re-enter our story in a most dramatic and unexpected way in thirteen years' time.

The reception Strauss received was a throwback to the old days: applause, cheers, encores. He was moving in the very highest circles of the English aristocracy, who took their lead from the queen herself. Such was his popularity with the upper classes that several members of the royal family and the nobility took it on themselves to organise a 'Farewell Matinée Musicale' at the end of the tour for Strauss's benefit 'as proof of their satisfaction of the admirable manner in which he has conducted the music at their balls and soirées this season'.

> *"Time has dealt kindly with him, for his broad, honest Teutonic face is still full of intelligence, and his fire and energy have not a jot abated."*
>
> The *Morning Post* on Strauss senior's final tour of England

The Duchesses of Gloucester, Cambridge and Mecklenburg-Strelitz personally undertook the sale of tickets. Strauss also paid a visit on the exiled Prince Metternich and his wife, no doubt reminiscing about the old days, and how things would never be the same again in Vienna.

Political events back home in Vienna seemed not to trouble Strauss's English hosts. The *Morning Post* reported with English *hauteur*:

> If the revolutionary mania of Austria has unsettled Germany, at least England has no reason to lament the political mischief …

And it found itself beguiled by the Viennese Waltz King:

> Time has dealt kindly with him, for his broad, honest Teutonic face is still full of intelligence, and his fire and energy have not a jot abated.

To some extent, though, the newspaper had allowed the dazzling exterior that Strauss wore like comfortable clothing to obscure the truth that lay beneath. Strauss remained depressed. Pained and tortured by the hostility shown towards him closer to home, he wrote anguished letters to close friends in Vienna. To Emilie he prophesied that this would be his last tour.

Once again, the strain of a relentless schedule, coupled with the chill and damp of the English climate, had affected his health. A flotilla of small boats that accompanied him and his orchestra as it sailed out of the Thames Estuary might have lifted his spirits temporarily, but it was an exhausted, depressed, unwell Johann Strauss who arrived back on 14 July at the small apartment in Vienna where, now a divorced man, he lived openly with Emilie and their five children.

Within days of his return, Strauss was back on the podium in front of his orchestra at Unger's Casino.[22] Legend has it that in the first piece, the overture to the new opera *Maritana* by William Vincent Wallace, Strauss's bow snapped. The audience gasped at this ill

---

[22] Some reports give the date as 15 July, the night after his return, though this seems unlikely.

omen. It is likely that the legend is an exaggeration. Maybe a string on his violin snapped. Maybe the ill omen came into being in the knowledge of what was to follow.

There are no reports, as far as I can tell, of how the performance went, what other pieces were played, whether Strauss was visibly unwell. What is certain, though, is that this was Johann Strauss's last concert.

In the late summer of 1849 the victorious Field-Marshal Radetzky returned from Italy to a hero's welcome from the old guard, who were once more in control after the failure of the street revolutions of the year before. A grand banquet in his honour was planned for

22 September in the Redoutensaal, the huge ceremonial hall of the Hofburg Palace, seat of the emperor.

Johann Strauss was engaged for the event. He and his orchestra were to provide suitable musical entertainment for the distinguished guests. Strauss would, naturally, perform his famous *'Radetzky March'*, as well as a newly commissioned work in the Field-Marshal's honour, the *'Radetzky-Bankett-Marsch'* ('Radetzky Banquet March').

But it was not to be. Strauss's health had worsened, and a telltale rash spreading across his body was diagnosed as scarlet fever. For the rest of her life Strauss's illegitimate daughter Clementina, eleven years old in the summer of 1849, blamed herself for passing on the scarlet fever that killed her father. But the fact that she survived, while her younger sister Maria did not, has led to suggestions that it might have been Strauss himself – given he was run down, depressed, generally unwell – who contracted the fever and passed it on to his children.

Early on the morning of 27 September, Anna Strauss, who it appears knew nothing of her ex-husband's illness, received news that he had died during the night. Her youngest son Eduard wrote many years later in strangely detached language that 'the poor deceased lay on wooden slats which had been taken from the bed and laid on the floor', and that Emilie had stripped the apartment in the Kumpfgasse of 'whatever could not be riveted or nailed firmly down'. A lengthy inventory of personal effects found in the apartment suggests this was at best an exaggeration.

Two days later members of Strauss's orchestra bore his coffin from the Kumpfgasse first to St Stephen's Cathedral for a funeral service, and from there to Döbling cemetery, where he was buried alongside his old friend and sometime foe, Joseph Lanner. A hundred thousand Viennese lined the funeral route.

The news was greeted with dismay in London. The *Illustrated London News* carried a lengthy obituary, in which it stated, 'Hosts of imitators have sprung up since Strauss, but to him will remain the glory of originality, fancy, feeling and invention.'

In Paris, Strauss's great admirer Hector Berlioz wrote his own tribute: 'Vienna without Strauss is like Austria without the Danube.'

Johann Strauss senior had led an extraordinary life. Born into comparative poverty in a tavern by the Danube, losing his father and mother tragically early, brought up by step-parents, he rose to be, in effect, an honorary member of the highest Viennese aristocracy. He had played before royalty and could number the likes of the Duke of Wellington, not to mention Queen Victoria, among his admirers.

His music, it is not an exaggeration to say, had changed Vienna for ever. It captured an era and achieved a popularity, not just in his home city but across Europe, that no other composer could equal.

But he had died, prematurely, at the age of forty-five. The way was now clear for his son, one month short of his twenty-fifth birthday, to take over where his father had left off. A young man spurred on by his father's opposition and intransigence, and who would go on to eclipse him totally.

Vienna now had just one Waltz King, one Johann Strauss.

Chapter Eight
A New Waltz King

his father? What if the orchestra was to disband, and they were to find themselves without regular employment?

A combination of Johann's humility and Amon's diplomacy seems to have done the trick. We can surely discount the story that members of the orchestra presented Strauss's baton on a cushion to his son. What is fact, though, is that the 'Orchestra of the late Strauss' elected Johann its leader, and on 7 October 1849, in the Kolonadensaal of the Volksgarten, Johann stood for the first time at the head of his father's orchestra. If any doubters still needed to be won over, that was achieved by Johann's decision to devote the concert entirely to works by his father.

Yet Johann Strauss II's rehabilitation was not entirely complete. Resentment of his revolutionary sympathies still existed at the very highest level. His father's death had left vacant the prestigious post of Music Director of Imperial Court Balls. Johann put himself forward, but was rejected. It went instead, on the recommendation of the emperor's parents no less, to one Philipp Fahrbach.

Johann, ever one to trim his sails according to prevailing winds, composed a patriotic march designed to praise the emperor himself, *Kaiser Franz Josef*. Several other compositions were similarly designed to flatter. Yet it was to be a further eleven years before he was finally elevated to the position his father had held.

This did not prevent Johann performing in the very highest circles. When Emperor Franz Josef met the Russian tsar, Nikolai the First, during an autumn festival in Warsaw, it was Johann and the Strauss Orchestra who provided musical entertainment. And though he did not yet officially hold the title, Johann was invited to conduct at a charity ball in the Redoutensaal of the Hofburg Palace during the Carnival of 1851 – a sign of the gradual softening of official policy towards him.

In these early years after his father's death, Johann found himself again and again compared to his famous father, and often unfavourably. It is true that as yet, musically speaking, his compositions did not rank with those of the elder Strauss, though that was soon to change. But for flamboyance and flair, and sheer magnetism on the podium, swaying with his violin under his chin, he was every bit the

Left
Franz Josef I, the new emperor of Austria who, in a life beset with tragedy, ruled the Habsburg Empire for sixty-eight years, living to see the First World War.

Above

Johann Strauss II with his orchestra, clad in the same bright uniform as his players, but indisputably the first among equals.

equal of his father. His younger years, sparkling eyes, thick black hair, soon made him the undisputed darling of Vienna.

In another way too, he was his father's son. He seemed to have an endless capacity for sheer hard work. He was churning out compositions at an extraordinary rate. By the time of the 1851 Carnival he had the best part of a hundred compositions to his name, and he was not yet twenty-six years of age.

In constant demand, Johann was called on to organise engagements, compose new pieces, arrange others, rehearse the orchestra, and frequently conduct at several different venues on the same day. It was his father all over again, and the effect it had on him was very similar.

Despite his youth, his energy was not limitless. He soon paid the price. At the end of February 1851, four months after his twenty-fifth birthday, he suffered a collapse. He was reported in early March to be 'dangerously ill' from typhoid and 'nervous fever'.

Amid a frenzy of speculation, one newspaper even reported the rumour that he had died.

In a further echo of his father, instead of convalescing he embarked on a concert trip to Germany, composing new pieces to take with him. This was soon followed by another concert tour through Prague, Leipzig, Berlin, Hamburg and Dresden.

Not surprisingly his health gave way again. This time it was more serious. He was unable to perform during the busy Christmas period of 1852. Several times, no doubt on his insistence, it was announced he was well enough to return to the podium, but each time it was postponed.

He did not return until six weeks later, and when he did it was characteristically with a vengeance. Two concerts back to back in different venues, with new compositions to premiere at each. When, on 18 February 1853, Emperor Franz Josef, strolling with a fellow officer on the Bastei, survived an assassination attempt – the sturdy high collar of his military uniform withstanding the knife of a Hungarian nationalist – Johann saw it as an opportunity to curry favour with the court, and composed his 'Kaiser Franz Josef I Rettungs-Jubel-Marsch' ('March of Rejoicing at the Deliverance of Emperor Franz Josef I').[23]

In the post-Metternich era, under a new emperor, Vienna was celebrating a new freedom. New dance halls were opening across the city, ever more grand and attracting more and more revellers. Johann and his orchestra were in demand everywhere. The rivalry with his father, the resentment towards him, were things of the past. Still from his father he retained one essential quality: the inability to say no.

Returning from a concert in the early hours of the morning, at the end of a day that had begun before dawn, Johann Strauss lost consciousness. This was followed by a nervous breakdown. At the age of twenty-seven he was very seriously ill.

This time there was no premature return to the podium. Johann's doctors ordered a prolonged stay at a sanatorium in

---

[23] The piece is typically upbeat, with the German national anthem sitting unsubtly at its heart. There is no record of whether the emperor appreciated the gesture.

Bad Gastein in the mountains south of Salzburg, followed by a further period of convalescence in Bad Neuhaus bei Cilli in southeast Austria.[24]

Crisis enveloped the Strauss family, the Strauss musical enterprise, in the Hirschenhaus. Step forward the matriarch of the family, Anna.

*   *   *

You can surely forgive Anna if she felt a certain amount of satisfaction, smugness even, in the way her family had turned out. She had been abandoned by her husband, her distress compounded by humiliation at her husband's open acknowledgement of a second family, her finances always difficult, the overt opposition of her husband to their eldest son's musical ambitions, the sheer emotional pain and the practical difficulty of having an estranged, difficult, uncooperative husband living in the same house.

What had she achieved in the face of all that? She had raised three sons and two daughters single-handed. One was proving himself to be a master musician, at least as good as his father and possibly better. And who could claim credit for that? Who was it who ignored the father's opposition and arranged for secret violin lessons for the boy?

The second son, Josef, had qualified as a mechanical engineer, achieving first-class grades in technical drawing and mathematics, and was now making headway in his chosen profession of architecture. Eduard, the youngest, was showing an aptitude for music, becoming a skilled harpist. Both daughters were attractive, lively, bright young women, and she had every reason to hope they would settle into good marriages.

The tribulations she had suffered had instilled in Anna a driving ambition for her brood. Her eldest son Johann was undoubtedly the family breadwinner. It was the Johann Strauss Orchestra that not only supported the whole family but allowed them to remain in the large, comfortable Hirschenhaus and live a lifestyle worthy of the city's most famous musical dynasty.

---

[24] Today Slovenia.

Now, for the first time since her husband's untimely – but probably not too unwelcome – death, the family enterprise was under threat. The new head of the household, the man on whom their continued existence depended, had succumbed to a debilitating illness, which had put him out of action.

Something needed to be done, and quickly. Anna knew what was called for. She discussed it with Johann, and he was in full agreement. It is possible he had already reached the same conclusion himself. The family business of music could not be allowed to falter. It needed someone new at its head, someone familiar with its ways, someone who could be relied on and trusted. It did not need at this stage to be permanent, but it would serve until Johann was fully recovered and could resume his duties.

The choice of person was obvious. Who knew Johann and his ways better than anyone? Who understood the tensions and difficulties that existed in the Hirschenhaus more intimately than any other? Who would have the interests of the family closest to his heart?

Josef Strauss the nascent architect. A Strauss himself. Anna and Johann laid out the situation before him. The future of the family, the future of the Johann Strauss Orchestra, lay in his hands. He needed to step forward and ensure the family's wellbeing.

The only problem was that Josef had never shown any interest in music. He was an engineer and would-be architect, not a musician. The family's musical business would have to get along without him.

He said no.

Chapter Nine
'Pepi' Joins the Family Firm

*J*osef was used to his own wishes being discounted by the family. Just as Strauss senior had tried to prevent his eldest son from pursuing a career in music, so he had early plans for Josef to enter the military. Josef reacted furiously, at the age of twenty-one banging off an angry letter to his father:

> *Leave me where I am; leave me what I am; don't snatch me away from a life that can bring me so many joys … Do not cast me into that rough, inconsistent world which destroys all feeling for humanity, a world for which I am not fitted, to which I was not born … I do not want to learn to* kill *people … I want to serve mankind as a human being …*

That letter pretty much summed up Josef, apart from the anger. He had a shy, gentle character, he was universally liked and content to make his own way in life without interference or influence from outside.

He had his way over his father, though less from the force of his argument than the fact that Strauss senior was about to leave on an extensive tour lasting the best part of a year and died shortly after his return.

Now, in 1853, as his elder brother lay ill on sick leave, Josef was attending courses on hydraulic engineering and water-works construction to work towards a diploma in engineering. In May he established his reputation as an innovative engineer by designing, with a colleague, a horse-drawn street-cleaning machine with rotating brushes. At first rejected as impractical, the Vienna

Municipal Council later realised its worth and the plans went into production.[25]

A quietly satisfied Josef began work on a snow-clearing machine, which was when his mother and elder brother told him they had other plans for him. He was needed as part of the Strauss musical enterprise. Josef was quietly defiant. He had seen his father off over plans to enter the military; he would do the same now.

Except that Anna and Johann knew exactly how to handle Josef: to appeal to his better nature, to explain to him that the welfare of the whole family – mother, brothers and sisters – depended on him, how they all looked to him to save them from destitution. As a clinching argument they stressed that it would be only a temporary arrangement, until Johann regained his health.

Josef could fight his uncaring father, but had no weaponry against his loved ones, those nearest and dearest to him. To the childhood friend he would marry in five years' time, Karoline Josefa Pruckmayer, he wrote on 23 July 1853, 'The unavoidable has happened; today I play for the first time at the Sperl … I wholeheartedly regret that this has happened so suddenly.'

'Suddenly' is the operative word. It had all happened so quickly that Josef had no time to become even passably efficient on the violin, so that he had to conduct at the Sperl with a baton – a severe break with Strauss tradition.

"Josef could fight his uncaring father, but had no weaponry against his loved ones, those nearest and dearest to him."

---

[25] Apart from obvious advances in technology, the basic design remains largely unchanged to this day.

Right

Josef Strauss;
his elder brother
Johann considered
him the more
gifted musician.

With characteristic dedication he took lessons in the violin and conducting, and even set about composing, mindful that each Strauss concert contained new pieces composed specially for the occasion.

The arts were not entirely alien to this talented engineer. For several years he had complemented his courses at the Polytechnic Institute with private tuition in drawing and painting at the Academy of Fine Arts. He had turned out many drawings, silhouettes, watercolours, all exhibiting great finesse and detail. He was accomplished in the literary field as well. He had written an anthology of poems, and an ambitious drama in five acts for which he wrote the text, visualised the settings and produced sketches of the characters, costumes and scenery.

By all accounts Josef – 'Pepi' to close friends and family – was a shy, sensitive man. The relatively few photographs of him show a gentle, almost soft, countenance, albeit with a firm gaze, prominent chin, and a characteristically Straussian full and flowing head of hair. He felt strongly enough about the upheavals of 1848 to join his elder brother on the barricades, even taking up arms, and at one point found himself the subject of an arrest warrant.

This seems to have been a passing phase, or rather a good example of that Viennese dual nature, crying on one side of the face and laughing on the other. A journalist described Josef as 'so audaciously stylish, so high-spiritedly Viennese when in cheerful company, and so artistically dreamy in the realm of music'.

We have no first-hand accounts of his debut with the Johann Strauss Orchestra at the Sperl, but he was soon booked to appear again – or, more accurately, had no choice but to fulfil his brother's next engagement, which was for the Parish Festival Ball in the Viennese suburb of Hernals on 29 August 1853.

This was the moment to find out if he had any talent at composing – I suspect as much for himself as for the orchestra and audience. He composed a piece to which he gave the opus number 1, and chose a title that intentionally left no one in any doubt that this was a temporary departure from his chosen career.

'Die Ersten und Letzten' ('The First and Last') is an extraordinary first work for a trained engineer in his mid-twenties. It begins with an uncharacteristically bold fanfare, for a shy man, repeated several times just in case you missed it. A slow introduction follows, a pause, and then comes a truly delightful passage in three-four time,

uprising, and with his father so often away on tour and at home with his mistress when he was in Vienna, it is unlikely that Eduard was able to develop a close relationship with him. Strauss senior died when Eduard was just fourteen.

Given this, I think we can also assume that Strauss senior was too uninterested and distracted to bother trying to dissuade his youngest son from a career in music, for this – remarkably – is what Eduard seems to have pursued. Anna must have been incredulous when it became obvious to her that Eduard, like his brothers, was extraordinarily gifted musically. All three sons, each of them highly talented musicians from an early age. Anna had had her revenge on her husband three times over!

In 1855, at the age of twenty, Eduard was playing harp in the Johann Strauss Orchestra. Vienna was now growing accustomed to seeing the three Strauss brothers all involved in the same enterprise, often appearing at the same venue together – or at least two out of the three – deputising for each other, and generally running light-music activities at the city's dance halls.

The Strausses – all three of them – were on the musical map, and it became obvious to them, and the people of Vienna, that they would never leave it. It was at about this time that Johann took to adopting the French version of his name, Jean.[27] Josef, as we have seen, was known as Pepi, and Eduard as Edi — later 'der schöne Edi' ('beautiful Edi') due to his good looks, coupled with a fondness for smart clothes and fashion.

With his two brothers now involved with the orchestra, Johann overcame his earlier doubts regarding Josef's commitment and accepted the invitation to Russia. The first concert at Pavlovsk was the best part of two years away, which would give him time to prepare and make sure that all was in place in Vienna before he left.

In the event the invitation to Russia was to prove far more of a commitment than he could possibly have imagined. It was to change his life, and not just musically. He would – as far as we know, for the first time – fall head over heels in love.

---

[27] He was not alone among composers for adopting more exotic forms of their names. Beethoven was fond of signing manuscripts and letters Louis or Luigi van Beethoven.

Chapter Ten
IN RUSSIA AND IN LOVE

*T*o say that the concerts went well in the summer of 1856 would be an understatement of huge proportions. At the opening concert in Pavlovsk on 18 May, which included pieces by Strauss father and son, as well as Verdi and Meyerbeer, there were so many demands for repeats and encores that the concert lasted until 1 a.m.

Word quickly spread. The aristocracy of St Petersburg made the train journey to Pavlovsk several times a week. It was soon impossible to get tickets at any price for a Strauss concert. It was reported that more than once, when a bell was sounded to announce the departure of the last train to the capital, the audience paid no attention, refusing to allow Strauss to stop, knowing it would mean camping down somewhere for the night away from home.

It was only a matter of time before the tsar himself, accompanied by members of the royal family, took their places in the imperial box. Once the tsar was seen to clap enthusiastically, there was not a single personage who did not follow his example. Johann Strauss, idol of Vienna, was soon known and lauded throughout Russia west of the Urals. His fame was truly international.

Hardly surprisingly, in the autumn of 1856 Strauss was signed up for the following two years. The demands on him were quite extraordinary. He was to give daily concerts from 2 May to 2 October with an orchestra of not less than thirty musicians. Daily concerts for five months – it's a schedule that would cause any of today's globe-trotting maestros or virtuosos to blanch. In fact it's unlikely any would agree to such a punishing schedule.

Nor was he totally free to select the music. He was to choose pieces from classical opera as well as garden and dance music, but

'in this he is to follow the taste of the local audience'. He would be expected to feature his own compositions, but 'he is also to perform the most popular and latest compositions of other famous masters, with a full orchestra under his personal direction'.

The remuneration, on the other hand, was exceedingly generous. He received 18,000 silver roubles for the five-month engagement each year, including his own and his orchestra's wages and travel costs.[28] He and his players also received free accommodation, and

[28] Around £90,000–£100,000 in today's money.

'If only my name was Olga.' Whether that was true or not, it is certain Strauss was aware of what wagging tongues were saying.

They were wagging closer to home too. It was widely believed matriarch Anna gave her eldest son a stern talking to, telling him to pull himself together. His brothers are certain to have taken the lead from their mother and given Johann some fraternal ribbing. For a man in his early thirties, criticism, even derision, from those closest to him might have been the most difficult to bear of all.

Johann Strauss was an artist, with an artist's sensibilities. He had been hurt; now he needed to get over it. In this painful task he received help from a totally unexpected source – Olga herself.

In the spring of 1859 a letter arrived in Vienna for Strauss. It was from Olga.

> *Do not condemn me when you read these lines. I will be brief and not embark on long explanation. I have been engaged for two weeks … Forget your unfaithful imp.*

And forget her he did. He returned for many more years to Pavlovsk, but there were no painful reunions, no secret meetings, no regrets. Olga Smirnitzky had dropped completely out of Johann Strauss's life.

But Strauss was not finished with love. At around the time he was pining for Olga in Vienna he was introduced to a singer renowned for her fine mezzo-soprano voice. Her name was Henriette Chalupetzky. It is possible, given her musical reputation and the frequency of her appearances on stage, that he made her acquaintance some years earlier. But it was only in the winter of 1861–2 that the relationship become something deeper.

It was as unlikely a liaison as that with Olga, although for very different reasons. Henriette was lauded for her performances across Europe, some critics even comparing her favourably with the Swedish Nightingale, the soprano Jenny Lind. Mendelssohn and Berlioz, no less, had dedicated songs to her.

But at a remarkably young age, somewhere in her early to mid-twenties, and already considerably wealthy, she gave it all up for an entirely different life – a somewhat colourful life, to put it

mildly. It's believed that in her twenties she bore no fewer than seven illegitimate children, the paternity of only two of whom is known.

At the age of twenty-five or thereabouts she became the mistress of the banker Moritz Todesco, a patron of the arts whose sumptuous house on the newly opened Ringstrasse abounded with artists, writers, musicians. It was there that Henriette played hostess to salon soirées, the baron's wife Sofie apparently complicit, willingly or otherwise.

If Henriette had ambitions to replace Sofie as baroness, she was to be disappointed. The baron was Jewish, Henriette Roman Catholic, and the law forbade persons of different religions to marry. Henriette was clearly not too upset though, since she remained Baron Todesco's mistress for a full eighteen years. Two of her children were his.

Then she met the most famous musician in Vienna, a friendship formed, and at some point it became intimate. They were in love, and Johann Strauss asked her to marry him. She was, technically, a free woman. The only potential problem was her relationship with the baron, but that proved not to be a problem at all. He understood entirely her nature, her artistic passion, and he consented totally to release her. He even consented to Henriette's request that he should keep custody of their two daughters so they could take his aristocratic title, allowing her access to them whenever she wished.

Henriette was free to marry Strauss. The path to marriage was not entirely smooth, however. Henriette's lifestyle was well known: her role as mistress, her illegitimate children, even her professional life as a singer was not regarded as an entirely wholesome career for a woman to pursue. Strauss encountered family opposition, most vocally from Josef, who was standing in for his elder brother in Pavlovsk when Johann announced his engagement. The quiet, reluctant musician conceded that Henriette was 'very well preserved', but knew of her reputation, adding that at forty-four she was seven years older than Johann. Matriarch Anna probably allowed herself to be persuaded by the fact that Henriette had a considerable fortune of her own, and was hardly likely to be a 'gold-digger'.

On 27 August 1862, in St Stephen's Cathedral in the heart of Vienna, Johann Strauss, 'Kapellmeister und Musikdirektor', married Henriette Chalupetzky, 'of single status'.

But Henriette Chalupetzky is not the name by which Strauss's bride is known to history. Early in her singing career she adopted the more exotic name of Jetty Treffz – the same Jetty Treffz who thirteen years earlier had shared the stage at London's Exeter Hall with Johann Strauss senior. What might he have thought then had he known that the singer on stage with him would one day marry his eldest son, making him her father-in-law?

Jetty Treffz was now Jetty Strauss. Johann Strauss the Younger, just two months short of his thirty-eighth birthday, was a married man. The extraordinary thing is that despite Jetty's exotic and uncertain past, despite the difference in age, despite family opposition and everything that seemed to mitigate against the marriage working, Johann Strauss could not have chosen a more suitable wife.

Chapter Eleven
TYING THE KNOT

Another, more historically significant, wedding had taken place in Vienna eight years earlier. It united two people totally unsuited to each other, temperamentally, emotionally, and even as first cousins genetically. It was a marriage that would be critically damaged by misunderstandings, divergent interests, absences and separation, and wounded beyond repair by suicide and murder.

On 24 April 1854, in St Augustine's Church alongside the imperial Hofburg Palace, Emperor Franz Josef married Elisabeth of Bavaria, known to history as Sisi. The emperor's accession to the imperial throne as a young man of eighteen, following the street revolution of 1848 and the enforced departure of Chancellor Metternich, ushered in a new era in every sense in Vienna.

A city that had been more or less in shutdown for more than thirty years revelled in its newfound gaiety. At last people could talk openly in the street, in cafés and in the back of horse-drawn cabs;[30] spies were a thing of the past; it was safe to go out at night; new dance halls opened and flourished; the waltz shook off any suspicion and the music of the Strauss family swept the city. Metternich was gone, there was a new young emperor on the throne. The refuge sought in cosy domesticity during the Biedermeier era was no longer required.

It was, admittedly, an earlier emperor who, responding to a proposal to construct licensed brothels, replied, 'The walls would cost me nothing, but the expense of roofing would be ruinous, for

---

[30] Known then and now as 'fiacres'.

it would be necessary to put a roof over the whole city,' but it might have applied just as aptly as Vienna entered the second half of the nineteenth century, and with considerably more openness.

The single most potent symbol of a new era dawning came about as a result of an order by the new emperor that the Bastei should be pulled down and replaced by a wide boulevard encircling the city.

This massive, metres-thick, city wall – so wide that a spacious walkway on top provided a fashionable area for people to stroll along, and for jugglers and street entertainers to ply their trade; so impenetrable that gates set into it at regular distances provided the only points at which it could be passed through – had been built nearly three centuries before, following the first Turkish invasion in 1529.

Now not only had the threat from the Ottoman empire dissipated, but Vienna was witnessing the most rapid expansion in its history. In under a decade in the mid-nineteenth century the population soared by 30 per cent. The city was spreading well beyond the city wall. Where once a few carriages might have clattered

along rarely frequented alleys, now there was all the bustle of a burgeoning city.

The Bastei had done its job. It had to go, and so Emperor Franz Josef – well aware he was upsetting the traditionalists – ordered its demolition. It was to be the largest building project in Vienna's history, turning the imperial capital into a vast building site. It was carried out carefully and painstakingly. Experts had to calculate exactly the right amount of explosives to demolish the wall, and not vast areas of the inner city with it.

In one way or another – a new building here or another one there – the work took more than two decades. But the all-important task, the demolition of the Bastei itself, symbol of Vienna's past, took seven years. On 1 May 1865 the emperor and his empress rode in a ceremonial carriage along the new boulevard (or at least that part of it that was complete) and officially declared it open.

The Ringstrasse, as it was named then and still is today, would come to encircle the inner city of Vienna. It soon became nearly two hundred feet wide, comprising a broad central section for carriages

Above

Vienna's Bastei being demolished, c. 1859.

and later vehicles, flanked by two tree-shaded lanes for horse riders, and ample pathways for promenaders under double rows of trees.

The city's largest and most imposing buildings began to be sited along the Ringstrasse. The first of these was the Opera House, soon followed by the Parliament building, the City Hall, the Stock Exchange, the Imperial Theatre.[31]

Vienna was changing. It was entering a new era, and there was no going back.

This was the Vienna in which Johann Strauss was making his name. His music – and to a lesser extent that of his brothers – symbolised the new era. It also encapsulated the mood of the Viennese, celebrating their liberty, their new ruler, a newly thriving economy. There was employment to be had, and when a day's work was done, what better entertainment than to go to one of the dance halls, eat and drink, and dance to Strauss?

As for the composer, demand for his music – and for the man himself – was so huge he simply could not keep up with it. He needed to make changes in order to cope. On 5 February 1861 it was announced: 'For the first time in Vienna. THREE BALLS IN ONE EVENING. Three large orchestras.'

Each one was a Strauss orchestra. How was this to be done? Johann took the decision to elevate his youngest brother Eduard to the podium. Each of the three brothers was now conducting a Strauss orchestra.

Still the toll on Johann was heavy. He was not just the most prolific composer: essentially he was running the whole enterprise. He also knew he was the one the audiences wanted to see. In 1862, preparing to leave for his seventh season in Pavlovsk, he received an offer to appear in Paris with his orchestra for three consecutive years for an annual fee of 100,000 francs. The work would simply not stop coming in. He turned it down, which just a few years earlier would have been unthinkable.

---

[31] To this day the Ringstrasse holds the most important buildings of government, the largest hotels, the most imposing shops.

Above
Vienna's Ringstrasse
holds some of the
city's most important
buildings, such as the
Imperial Theatre.

While in Pavlovsk Johann Strauss fell ill again. It was an intermittent ailment and the doctors did not make a diagnosis. Strauss handed conducting duties over to a deputy, to the disappointment of audiences. In July he wired home for Eduard to take over from him. Anna intervened and insisted Josef should go instead.

Josef was angry. A reluctant musician in the first place, he objected to having his life disrupted at the whim of his elder brother. Once in Pavlovsk, and sharing conducting duties with Johann on the first night, he was resentful and deeply suspicious. On the morning Johann left for home, Josef wrote to his wife, 'He was more fresh and healthy than ever before. This time he has fooled physicians, doctors, everybody.'

He might well have been right. Strauss was clearly tired, if not close to exhaustion, but fundamentally it seems there was nothing wrong with him. Exactly three weeks after leaving Russia, Johann Strauss was well enough to marry Jetty Treffz.

The newest member of the Strauss family now proved herself to be not just a deeply caring wife, but also a highly efficient organiser. As one modern biographer puts it, Jetty became the complete companion for her husband – 'wife, lover, artistic

and to the north the city itself with the spire of St Stephen's Cathedral rising from its centre.

It was a two-storey mansion, which Jetty was to furnish in elaborate style, and one can forgive her a touch of *lèse-majesté* in her description of it, written in October 1868:

> *Johann has bought a small house here, so really nice and comfortable that we imagine we are living in dear Albion [England]. Opposite us is the Schönbrunn botanical garden, and the inside of our house is lovely.*

Even before the move, in a happy marriage with onerous duties lifted from his shoulders, Strauss's creative juices were flowing. The magnificent *'Geschichten aus dem Wienerwald'* ('Tales from the Vienna Woods') dates from this period, with its famous solo on Austria's national instrument, the zither.

He also composed what could be said to be his first truly great waltz, *'Morgenblätter'* ('Morning Papers'), all the more extraordinary when you consider he gave it the opus number 279 – in other words nearly 300 pieces already composed, and literally hundreds more still to come.[33]

'Morgenblätter' was written to a commission from the organising committee of the Concordia Ball, which was staged annually by a society of Austrian journalists (and given its appropriate title by them).

Strauss received another commission at around this time, from the Wiener Männergesang-Verein (Vienna Men's Chorus). It is slightly surprising that Strauss accepted the commission, given the fate of his last commission from them. It was good that he did so, however, as it resulted in another of Strauss's best waltzes, *'Wein, Weib und Gesang!'* ('Wine, Woman and Song!').[34]

The slightly earlier commission has an interesting history. The society asked Strauss to compose a choral work for them. Strauss accepted, despite the fact he was unused to writing for voices. Maybe he relished the challenge. Maybe Jetty did not, because for the best part of two years he did nothing about it.

He finally produced a new waltz for them for unaccompanied voices – actually four waltz numbers with introduction and brief

---

[33] This is arguably the largest output of quality pieces in the history of classical music, possibly equalled only by the German Baroque composer Telemann.

[34] The exclamation mark is a particularly Straussian touch.

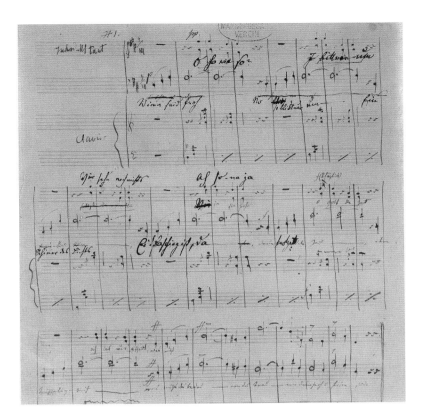

coda – using words written by one of the chorus members, who fancied himself a poet. He then sent a hastily written piano accompaniment, with a note of apology: 'Please excuse the poor and untidy handwriting – I was obliged to get it finished within a few minutes. Johann Strauss.' (Is it too fanciful to imagine him scribbling this note down quickly while Jetty was out of the room?) Even closer to the first performance he provided an orchestral accompaniment.

Strauss was not present when the men's choir performed it, having conducting duties elsewhere, but was said to be seriously disappointed at its apparently poor reception. Actually several newspaper critics wrote the next day that the piece was 'splendid', 'catchy', 'lovely'. But it is surely a measure of just how popular Strauss's music was that the fact that the choral piece received just a single encore amounted to a failure.

Strauss put it to one side with a shrug, apparently saying to Josef, 'To hell with the waltz. I am only sorry about the coda. I thought that would be a success.'

More important matters loomed. Strauss had been invited to the most cosmopolitan, exciting, lively city in Continental Europe. His father might have performed in Paris thirty years earlier, but Johann Strauss the Younger never had. In the summer of 1867 that changed.

The Paris engagement did not begin well. In the first place Strauss had to engage an entirely new orchestra, since his own had commitments in Vienna. Secondly there were general complaints that Strauss played the waltz too quickly, making it difficult to dance to. Most detrimental of all, Paris was staging a World Exhibition: Strauss was merely one of many attractions.

Everything changed when the newspaper *Le Figaro* not only praised Strauss and his music, but began to champion it and recommend it day after day. It had the desired effect. Jetty was soon able to write home:

> *The receipts have increased* every *day and the public is so frantically aflame for Jean that I cannot find words to depict* this *enthusiasm … they are simply crazy for this Viennese music.*

Strauss was suddenly in such demand that he had to find new material, and quickly. One of the pieces he remembered was the set of waltzes he had written for the Vienna Men's Chorus. He had not played it since, so no one in the Paris audience could have heard it before.

He wired home to Vienna and asked for the parts to be sent to him. Swiftly he orchestrated the piece, doing away with the voices, and performed it to a packed house.

Strauss retained the title of the poem that had been the original inspiration for the piece, *'An der schönen blauen Donau'* ('By the Beautiful Blue Danube'). This time it received encore after encore. Word spread faster than a forest fire.

Back in Vienna the soft copper plates used by Strauss's publishing house wore out after producing 10,000 copies. Before the first print run was over, a hundred sets of plates had been worn out.

Johann Strauss had produced his most popular and enduring composition. He was now truly at the very pinnacle of his fame, the Strauss musical dynasty dominating music across Europe.

Things literally could not get better for the Waltz King. But they could get worse. The Strauss family enterprise was soon to endure its own *annus horribilis*.

Chapter Twelve

THE STRAUSS FAMILY
IN MOURNING

At the Polish border customs officials refused to allow musical instruments, as well as sheet music, through. That was eventually solved, but on arrival in Warsaw the promised accommodation was unavailable. Far more important than these hitches was the fact that a number of musicians failed to arrive in Warsaw, due to a mix-up on the part of the musical agents.

Everything had to be delayed. Josef wired frantically to Eduard to send musicians from Vienna, at the same time scouring Warsaw for local talent. On 17 May, two days after the scheduled opening concert, Josef wrote to Johann:

> *I am disconsolate. No prospect of beginning. When this letter has reached your hands, the catastrophe will have reached its highest peak.*

Little did Josef know what an understatement that would be.

The first concert finally took place on 22 May, and was well received. Five days later Josef cancelled his subsequent appearance because he was unwell. He next stood in front of the orchestra on 1 June.

Things seemed to be going well until it came time to play Josef's latest composition, a medley entitled *'Musikalisches Feuilleton'* ('Musical Supplement').[35] In a particularly tricky passage, strings and wind began to pull apart.

Josef gestured frantically, trying to give the beat, but the orchestral sections pulled further apart. With unerring inevitability, the piece was coming off the rails. Josef suddenly staggered, lost his footing, fell from the podium, and cracked his head as he tumbled to the floor.

Bleeding from the nose and ears, he was carried back to his apartment. His wife Karoline rushed to Warsaw, where she found Josef with 'his limbs paralysed, scarcely able to speak', as Eduard later wrote.

Johann, accompanied by Jetty, followed, but not until the end of the month. He himself was in poor health (again). This time he was suffering from jaundice. In the first week of July doctors in Warsaw were attending to both Johann and Josef Strauss.

Johann was well enough to lead the orchestra at three concerts later in that first week. Josef's condition, by contrast, had not improved.

---

[35] Unpublished and now lost.

Karoline decided to move Josef back to Vienna, where medicine was more advanced and there would be no language problems.

The two-day carriage journey can only have exacerbated Josef's illness. On arrival in Vienna his condition was clearly critical. Doctors diagnosed a probable brain tumour, which would have accounted for the fainting spells, as well as the sudden loss of consciousness on the podium.

On the afternoon of 22 July 1870, one month short of his forty-third birthday, Josef died. Doctors asked permission of Karoline to carry out a post-mortem so they could establish if suspicions of a brain tumour were correct, but Karoline was adamant in her refusal. Accordingly the inquest found that Josef had died of 'decomposition of the blood', and the true cause of his tragically early death will never be known.

Josef was buried alongside his mother in the Strauss family grave in the St Marx Cemetery outside the city boundary of Vienna.[36] Once again, as with their mother, Johann Strauss did not attend the funeral.

Patrick Sarsfield Gilmore who invited Johann Strauss and his orchestra to perform in Boston and New York.

⁓⧢

The decade that began with trauma for Johann Strauss would have more shattering news for him before it was finished, but in the year following the double deaths in the family he was distracted by a visit from an Irish-born composer by the name of Patrick Sarsfield Gilmore.[37]

Gilmore had been put in charge of organising the World's Peace Jubilee and International Music Festival planned for the following summer in Boston. Everything about it was to be big. It would feature massive ensembles made up of several bands, and two huge coliseums were to be specially built, one holding 60,000, the other 120,000. Gilmore wanted, as his star turn, the Johann

---

[36] Where, seventy-nine years earlier, Mozart had been buried in a common grave. The cemetery was closed to burials in 1874, but restored in the early twentieth century and opened to the public.

[37] Best known for writing the lyrics to the American Civil War song 'When Johnny Comes Marching Home'.

Right

Johann Strauss liked to compose standing at a desk. This hand-coloured lantern slide shows him on the verandah of his country house in Bad Ischl in 1880 (see page 194).

Strauss Orchestra with its founder at its head.[38] After Boston, Gilmore assured Strauss he would arrange dates in New York, to increase his popularity even more, as well as bringing in considerably increased fees.

If there was just one market left for Strauss to conquer, it was the United States, and what a market it could be. Huge audiences guaranteed, fees that in Europe Strauss could only dream of, and the final cementing of him as a *world*-renowned musician.

Which makes it all the more surprising that he had no desire to go. The reason gives us an insight into Strauss's character. In fact the whole trip – which he finally agreed to under pressure from Jetty, which lasted less than a month, and of which he hated every minute – gives us perhaps the most complete picture we have of Strauss as a man, thanks to the diligence of the American press.

I have already described Strauss's fear and detestation of anything to do with death. Well, he had a morbid fear of any activity that could lead to it too, and that included a sea voyage across the Atlantic. Accordingly, on 19 May 1872, two weeks before the planned departure, Strauss drew up his Last Will and Testament, naming his wife as his sole heir and main beneficiary.[39]

He expressed this fear of death, albeit in somewhat laconic tones, to Gilmore himself as one of the reasons for his initial refusal to go. 'And what happens when your Indians massacre me?' he asked.[40]

Once in New York he addressed the possibility of a violent end in an interview with a reporter from the *Sun* newspaper: 'I want to mention something else to you that is perfectly awful, monstrous. There are no *Fahnwächter* [flagmen] on the railroads here. It is perfectly monstrous.'

Jetty, in the hotel room for the interview, confirmed Strauss's fear. 'My husband says he'd rather be killed swiftly, and be done with it,

---

[38] He also invited Giuseppe Verdi, who – busy preparing *Aida* for its world premiere in Cairo – turned him down.

[39] Maybe he realised his fear was unnecessary, since he knew perfectly well Jetty would be travelling with him.

[40] A fear not entirely without substance. Europe was awash with stories about encounters between settlers and Native Americans, and while Strauss was in America at least two massacres occurred.

This single interview, published in the *Sun of New York* on Saturday, 13 July 1872, I find utterly compelling. It tells us more about Johann Strauss the man than any number of musicological treatises on his compositions. What a beguiling image it conjures up of the most popular composer and orchestral leader *in the world* walking along the streets of New York in foul mood, wishing he had never come, disgusted at the price of getting a shave, with not even the satisfaction of a decent beer with which to cheer himself up!

He claimed to his interviewer that he was charmed by New York – though that is more likely to have been intended to flatter the journalist, particularly given his views on shaving and beer – and one wonders whether his opinions might have been improved a mere decade or so later, when the first skyscrapers went up, followed by the iconic Statue of Liberty.

Musically his performances were a triumph, but not to him. He was not particularly impressed that US President Ulysses S. Grant attended the afternoon concert at the Peace Jubilee in Boston on Tuesday 25 June (he was well used to playing before royalty and heads of state). And as for the performances he gave in the larger of the city's two new coliseums, the one holding 120,000 people, don't believe a word of what he wrote to the *Neue Freie Presse* in Vienna, extolling 'my joyful experience in this extraordinary affair'.

The truth came in a letter he later wrote to a friend. He uses coruscating language, criticising every aspect of these gigantic performances, and using considerable exaggeration for effect. This is the same Strauss angry at the cost of a shave, disgusted at the taste of beer, wishing he had never made the journey to the United States. He obviously feels his initial instincts not to go were correct. Clearly nothing anybody could do – including Jetty – to cheer him up was successful. He must have been a difficult man to deal with in those few short weeks.

That letter, which so perfectly captures his stubbornness and irascibility, is worth quoting in full:

> *On the concert platform were thousands of singers and instrumentalists, and I had to conduct them! A hundred assistant conductors had been placed at my disposal to control these gigantic masses, but I was only able to see those nearest to me. Although we had rehearsed, an artistic performance, a proper production, was unthinkable. I would have put my life at risk if I had refused to appear … Suddenly a cannon fired, a gentle hint for us twenty thousand to begin the concert. 'The Beautiful Blue Danube' was on the programme. I gave the signal, my hundred sub-conductors followed me as quickly and as well as they could, and then a fearful racket broke out that I shall never forget as long as I live! As we had begun more or less together, my whole attention was now directed towards seeing that we should also finish together. Thank Heaven, I also managed that. The hundred thousand-strong audience roared their approval, and I breathed a sigh of relief when I found myself in the fresh air again and felt the firm ground beneath my feet. The next day I had to flee an army of impresarios, who promised me the whole of California for a tour of America. I had already had quite enough of the so-called music festival, and returned to Europe with the very greatest possible speed.*

Curmudgeonly to the end!

Among the favourites Strauss performed in the US was, as he stated in that letter, *'By the Beautiful Blue Danube'* ('The Blue Danube

"The US sojourn was a triumph. Strauss's worldwide fame was assured. Yet he looked back on it as a disaster."

Madness', as the *Sun* described it) as well as *'Artist's Life'*, *'1001 Nights'*, *'New Vienna'*, *'Pizzicato-Polka'*, and several specially written new compositions including a waltz that featured *'The Star-Spangled Banner'* in its coda.

The US sojourn was a triumph, and earned Johann Strauss a small fortune. His worldwide fame was assured. Yet he looked back on it for the rest of his life as a disaster, something he wished he had never done. Many times in later years he was invited back, with ever more enticing offers. But he meant what he said in that letter. He never returned.

Chapter Thirteen
STRAUSS TURNS HIS HAND TO OPERETTA

which was a favourite of Beethoven's and had seen the premiere of many of his works, including the first version of his only opera *Fidelio*, but which now specialised in lighter musical theatre – entered into a charming conspiracy with Jetty.

He persuaded her to steal some of her husband's manuscripts. He then employed librettists to put words to the pieces. One morning a group of singers turned up at the Strausses' house in Hietzing, gathered round the piano, and sang Strauss's music to him, with words. Given that, as far as I am aware, none of these vocal versions has survived, the story is unlikely to be true. But its existence attests to the efforts that were being made to persuade Strauss to attempt operetta, and Jetty's leading role in the persuasion.

Whatever the tactics, Strauss respected his wife's business and artistic acumen, and some time in the early 1860s he began to compose operetta.

Word quickly spread about this new direction, but Strauss was not saying a word. He rebuffed all attempts to make him talk about it. He knew he needed to learn a new art form, and that it would be a struggle. He wanted to be left alone while he turned his hand to it.

He did not underestimate the challenge. Despite the Viennese newspapers announcing in January 1864 that Strauss would soon produce his first stage work, his first two attempts – *Don Quichotte* and *Romulus* – were stillborn. Strauss had actually completed two acts of *Romulus* before abandoning it. Things were not going well for him in the field of operetta.

Strauss was content to put operetta to one side while he concentrated on appearances in Pavlovsk and a full concert schedule at home. Then in October 1868 Jetty let the cat out of the bag by writing to a friend that Johann had declined offers to appear in Frankfurt, London and America, because he wanted to spend the winter 'working on an opera for the Wiedner Theatre'.[42]

The newspapers soon knew about it, and on 6 November 1868 *Die Presse* announced that Strauss was near to completing an operetta which he had entitled *Die lustigen Weiber von Wien* ('The Merry Wives of Vienna').

---

[42] The old name for the Theater an der Wien.

Above

Theater an der Wien,
hand-coloured lantern
slide, c. 1890; away from
the formalities of the
state-run theatres, it
became the centre of
Viennese operetta, seeing
the premiere of Strauss's
Die Fledermaus and *Der
Zigeunerbaron*.

He certainly was. It premiered soon after, and vanished soon after that. But Strauss had caught the bug, or more likely Jetty kept up an encouragement offensive, greatly helped by an amazing deal that was on offer. In return for signing an exclusive contract with the Theater an der Wien for the seasons 1870–1 and 1871–2, Strauss was offered a raft of benefits, of which the most attractive was a guaranteed 10 per cent share in the profits on the *gross* receipts of each performance.

There was no way Jetty was going to let him turn that down. And so he tried again, this time with the story of Ali Baba, which premiered to a full house on 10 February 1871 as *Indigo und die vierzig Räuber* ('Indigo and the Forty Thieves').

to America, and much further afield to Australia. In December 1876 it became the first Strauss operetta to be performed in London, and the following year it reached Paris.[46]

A number of years later, in 1894, *Die Fledermaus* was to receive its highest musical compliment. That *über*-serious, deeply emotional composer Gustav Mahler, in his capacity as music director of the staid, conservative, traditional Vienna Court Opera, introduced the 'operetta of all operettas' into the repertoire.

It played to packed houses, but there is a suggestion that even an admirer such as Mahler felt it a shame that Viennese audiences seemed to favour operetta over more heavyweight opera. This was, after all, the city of Mozart, Beethoven, Schubert, Brahms – and, albeit briefly, Wagner.

After a sell-out on a hot August day, Mahler said to a colleague:

> *Excellent [that it's a sell-out], but it's* Fledermaus *instead of* Walküre, *which I gave the night before last. I value* Fledermaus *and am pleased that it brings in money, but it is nonetheless sad that* Fledermaus *packs the house, and not* Walküre.

So what is it about *Die Fledermaus*, which seemed to come out of nowhere after a string of failed attempts, even flops, from Strauss that makes it the best-loved, most enduring of all Viennese operetta, to the extent that the *still* conservative and traditional Vienna State Opera stages a new production every New Year's Eve?

It is, of course, light-hearted, even superficial, with an utterly implausible plot. But then what operetta does not fit that description? Above all, it is *fun*. I have been known to sit through an entire production with a smile from ear to ear that never fades. Its centrepiece is a boisterous party, a ball. The first act leads up to it, and the third act unravels the knotty relationships that are formed at the event.[47]

Left

The best-known numbers from *Die Fledermaus* arranged by Johann Strauss for piano to be danced as a quadrille, which regularly happens at the New Year's Day Grand Viennese Ball.

---

[46] Substantially revised and under a new title, *La Tzigane* ('The Gypsy Girl').

[47] Modern directors delight in putting star turns into Count Orlofsky's ball, characters who otherwise take no part in the performance. In 1990 the great Australian soprano Dame Joan Sutherland was joined on stage at Covent Garden by tenor Luciano Pavarotti and mezzo-soprano Marilyn Horne for several numbers to mark her retirement.

fuelled by the success of *Die Fledermaus* – was undimmed, and Jetty was unstinting in her encouragement.

While Strauss was in Paris conducting at the new Paris Opéra, clearly longing to return to Jetty and their home in Hietzing, Jetty wrote to a friend on 20 October 1877, 'Jean is being drawn to Hietzing by his work desk – where, waiting longingly for him, is "Blinde Kuh".'

But Jetty was never to see this new operetta. On 8 April 1878 she suffered a heart attack and at 11.30 p.m. she died.

Chapter Fourteen
JOHANN STRAUSS TASTES FAILURE

*I*n eight short years Johann Strauss had lost his mother, his brother and his wife. His reaction each time seemed to surpass what was normal. Grief is one thing, but Strauss's behaviour bordered on the irrational. His morbid fear of anything to do with death led him to stay away from the funerals of his mother and brother, as I have recounted. Now, once again, his reaction was extreme.

He not only refused to attend Jetty's funeral, he adamantly refused to have anything to do with arranging it. As with the previous two deaths in the family, his younger brother Eduard was left to make all the arrangements. This was such a clear abrogation of duty that it caused considerable antagonism on Eduard's part.

Johann went further. The same night he found Jetty's lifeless body, he fled the house in Hietzing that was their home and never set foot inside it again. He took refuge in Eduard's house and told him he wanted nothing to do with what now needed to be done. Eduard was left to pick up the pieces. It was Eduard who had the body taken away, Eduard who arranged the funeral, walked behind the coffin, and dealt with the legal formalities.

Johann, we know, had a horror of death and everything associated with it, but in this case it might have been exacerbated by the unquestionable fact that his marriage had been running into trouble. The seven-year age gap began to show as Strauss turned fifty years of age, and Jetty drew closer to sixty. Her health had not been good for some time. She was prone to speak of herself as 'a poor old cripple', and infirmity had robbed her of her looks, and to a certain extent her charm. Her ill health cannot have helped marital relations and might even have contributed to their deterioration.

There was also the issue of her complicated former life. It is possible Strauss was aware only of the two illegitimate daughters Jetty had by Baron Todesco, and not of the five others. Certainly he was taken totally by surprise when, in the autumn of 1876, a young man turned up at the Hietzing house, addressed Jetty as 'mother', and asked for money.

Strauss threw him out of the house, but the man then wrote to his mother asking for money, making increasingly unreasonable demands. On the day of her death she received a letter from her son that apparently amounted to blackmail. Strauss had no hesitation in saying it was the shock of this letter that induced the fatal heart attack.

It had been an open secret in Viennese musical circles for some time that the Strausses' marriage had become rocky, and Strauss was known to have developed a roving eye. It had roved particularly towards a young actress by the name of Angelika Dittrich, who had come to Vienna in search of a theatrical career.

wife moved into the newly completed mansion on the Igelgasse in an exclusive district of Vienna.[53]

The reception room was everything Jetty had wanted it to be, and here Strauss entertained such eminent musical guests as Johannes Brahms, Anton Bruckner and Giacomo Puccini. A contemporary print shows Strauss seated at a large ornate desk, dressed in a sharply cut and immaculately tailored suit, a bearskin rug under his feet, and a tasteful nude painting on the wall.

These names and this lifestyle were totally unfamiliar to Lili. She was out of her depth and out of her class, and that twenty-five-year age gap must have weighed on her heavily. Matters were not helped – in fact they were considerably exacerbated – when Strauss's newly completed and much awaited new operetta, *Blinde Kuh*, premiered on 18 December 1878, less than seven months after Strauss and Lili were married.

Lili no doubt enjoyed a glittering evening at the Theater an der Wien, where all the talk was of the brilliant and charismatic Alexander Girardi in the principal role. The combination of Strauss and Girardi. What could possibly go wrong?

Everything. In fact there had been an ominous piece of bad luck in the run-up to the premiere. Several numbers Strauss had already composed were lost in the move to the new mansion. He was forced to compose twelve new numbers. Is it too fanciful to imagine him furiously accusing Lili of mislaying them, of not looking after his precious manuscripts properly, as Jetty surely would have done?

The operetta was a huge flop, in fact the only complete failure of his career, humiliatingly withdrawn after only sixteen performances. He could take small comfort that the inane libretto by one Rudolf Kneisel took most of the blame. Reviews were excoriating – 'Among his other talents, Johann Strauss also possesses that of selecting the worst possible text', and (the pun working in English as well as German), 'Johann Strauss personally conducts – the audience to the outside of the theatre.'[54]

[53] Today the Johann-Strauss-Gasse.

[54] As always Strauss knew better than to waste a good tune. He reused several pieces from *Blinde Kuh*, most successfully the waltz *'Kennst du mich?'*, which was played by salon orchestras for decades afterwards.

Strauss had a secure enough reputation to survive a flop, particularly when it was the librettist who took most of the criticism. But it was another nail in the already fragile coffin that was his marriage to Lili.

His next operetta, the seventh, *Das Spitzentuch der Königin* ('The Queen's Lace Handkerchief'), received an opening-night ovation greater than any since *Die Fledermaus*, but fickle as these things are, it swiftly disappeared into obscurity, possibly sped on its way by the fact that at least four librettists, and subsequently even more, claimed a share of the profits, resulting in a messy court case.[55]

A similar fate befell the eighth, *Der lustige Krieg* ('The Merry War'), praised in the *Neue Freie Presse* as 'the work of a brilliant talent', but on this occasion the cause might have been something entirely unrelated, which devastated the city and changed Viennese theatrical life.

Less than two weeks after the opening of *Der lustige Krieg*, on 7 December 1881, the Ringtheater, one of the most imposing buildings on the still newly completed Ringstrasse, presented the German-language premiere of Offenbach's hugely popular *Hoffmanns Erzählungen* ('The Tales of Hoffmann').

The following night, brilliant reviews combined with a public holiday ensured a full house. Minutes before the curtain rose, an ignition fault with the gas lighting backstage started a fire. It quickly spread unchecked across the auditorium, engulfing the audience. In total 386 people died in a tragedy unprecedented of its kind in the city's history.

In the long term it led to a complete overhaul of safety in theatres, with new and stricter regulations. In the short term people simply stayed away. A measure of Strauss's popularity is that *Der lustige Krieg*, playing at the Theater an der Wien, seemed to buck the trend, running for more than a hundred consecutive performances before it faded into relative obscurity.

In the previous year Strauss had purchased an imposing country retreat at Schönau-bei-Leobersdorf about twenty miles south-west of Vienna, to give him peace and quiet and an escape from the

"It transpires that Strauss might not only have been aware of his wife's infidelity but might not have been entirely faithful himself."

---

[55] Strauss once again used the best material from it, fashioning it into one of his most popular waltzes, *'Rosen aus dem Süden'* ('Roses from the South').

Left

On the night of 7 December 1881, fire engulfed the Ringtheater, leading to a complete overhaul of safety regulations in theatres.

city and even from the house in Igelgasse, where he was constantly called on by visitors.

Musically speaking it was an inspired move; on a personal level a disaster. Strauss composed his two most popular operettas after *Die Fledermaus* at Schönau – *Eine Nacht in Venedig* ('One Night in Venice') and *Der Zigeunerbaron* ('The Gypsy Baron') – but it took him away from the city, the social whirl and the bright lights. Good for Strauss, not so good for his wife.

Lili still harboured ambitions to pursue a career in theatrical management. In May 1880 the director of the Theater an der Wien, Maximilian Steiner, died and his son Franz took over.

Lili knew father and son well from their dealings with Strauss – in fact Max Steiner is often credited for the making of Strauss as a composer of operetta. Whereas Steiner senior was a serious and dedicated theatre manager, whose premature death was said to have been brought on by the precarious finances of the theatre, his son was in another mould. A sole photograph shows an unsmiling young man, but with tousled dark hair and fashionable pencil moustache, and a bow tie tied at a louche angle. It is easy to imagine the face breaking into spontaneous laughter.

It is not exactly clear when Lili began an affair with Franz, but it was certainly under way in 1882, two years after the purchase of the villa in Schönau, when Lili was thirty-two years of age and Steiner three years younger.

It appears Strauss knew what was going on and did his best to win his wife back. On 28 July he wrote an imploring letter to her while she was in Franzensbad – whether with Steiner we do not know. The tone is not that of a world-famous musician at the height of his career and creative powers, more that of a lovelorn cuckold: 'Let yourself be well and truly kissed, dear Lili, but do not run away from me! Please stay!'

The language suggests he was even prepared to allow the affair to continue, as long as Lili stayed with him. She did not. She moved first into the Theater an der Wien with Steiner, achieving her ambition of helping him to run the theatre, then followed him to Berlin, where she leaves our story.[56]

Despite that letter, it transpires that Strauss himself might not only have been aware of his wife's infidelity but – as in his first marriage – might not have been entirely faithful himself.

In early November 1882, just four months after imploring Lili to stay with him, Strauss left Berlin, where he had been conducting *Der lustige Krieg*, for Pest to conduct the same operetta there. He did not travel alone. Accompanying him was a widow aged twenty-six – thirty-one years his junior – by the name of Adèle Strauss.

---

[56] In Berlin Lili and Steiner separated, and she ran her own photographic studio, 'Atelier Lili'. She later returned to Austria (though not Vienna), where she opened another studio. During the First World War she fostered two daughters abandoned by their mother and whose father had been sent to the Front. Lili often said she wished she had not left Strauss. Her foster daughters were fond of her, erecting a gravestone on her death in 1919, which read, 'Your goodness is not forgotten.'

Chapter Fifteen
TO THE ALTAR AGAIN

*J*ohann Strauss had known Adèle for the best part of eight years, for the simple reason that after she married one Anton Strauss (no relation to the musical Strausses, the name was a complete coincidence) she moved into the rooms he occupied in the Hirschenhaus, the same capacious house into which Johann Strauss the elder had moved his growing family many decades before. The Strauss family had long since moved out, but Anton's father had acted as financial adviser to them, and it is likely there will have been meetings, or at least social gatherings, at the Hirschenhaus.

What is certain is that Johann Strauss and Adèle knew each other, and Adèle had frequently let Johann know she admired both him and his music. It was therefore natural, when Anton died suddenly after less than three years of marriage, leaving Adèle with a two-year-old daughter, that she would turn to Johann Strauss for comfort and advice.

A mutual attraction developed, and swiftly turned into something more. Johann declared his love for Adèle, deciding he wanted to spend the rest of his life with her, and she was eager to reciprocate.

It is worth pausing for a moment to look at how unlikely a match this was. Johann Strauss, now aged fifty-seven, married twice before, no children, world-famous composer and orchestral leader, and Adèle, aged twenty-six, widowed with a small child.

A cynic might say they each had plenty to gain, with an obvious affection for each other but no question of love. After all, they could be father and daughter. It is true there was mutual benefit. For Johann there was once again companionship, with the hope that – if the gods were smiling – Adèle might be able to organise his diary, keep house so he could devote himself to his music, generally look after him.

For Adèle, well, it would have been hard to resist Johann's gesture of love – an irrevocable annuity for life of 4000 gulden (roughly equivalent to £11,000 today). Also she must have known that a widow with a small child would be unlikely to attract an admiring young suitor. In these circumstances, when a comfortable and secure life beckoned, the enormous age difference was nothing more than a minor issue for her.

All true, but let us wind fast forward many years and see what actually happened. In the first place Johann and Adèle stayed together until Johann died seventeen years later in her arms. In the interim she more than filled the void left by Jetty, providing him with perfect conditions in which to work. In fact progress on *Eine Nacht in Venedig*, which had stalled due to domestic tensions with Lili, resumed and Strauss swiftly brought it to completion. The autograph score shows that Adèle herself copied out parts of the song texts. She was the perfect successor to Jetty, and more.

Johann's transformation, once Adèle moved into the house on the Igelgasse, was noticed by everyone. Friends commented that he had shed years, with the energy of a man half his age. It was now he began to dye his hair and moustache black, augmenting the youthful look. It was even rumoured he took to riding his horses at Schönau, which toned him up physically.

If anyone doubted Johann was in love, we have written proof. Almost daily he wrote her little love notes. On one occasion before going to the theatre to conduct, he left her a note saying, 'My dear Adèle! I shall change the tempo from *maestoso* to *allegro* so I can hurry

"My dear Adèle! I shall change the tempo from maestoso to allegro so I can hurry back to you all the sooner."

Johann Strauss

Right

Johann Strauss and his
third wife, Adèle. Despite
an age difference of more
than thirty years, it was
a very happy marriage,
lasting until Strauss's death
seventeen years later.

back to you all the sooner and kiss you a few minutes earlier. Your Jean.' On another occasion: 'You are the queen of my happiness, of my life!' And again, when he was away in Berlin: 'Cherchez la femme. Sleep well, you black-eyed Adèle, the only woman on earth.' In what is quite possibly a rare acknowledgement of his age, one note read, 'Let us be merry, Adèle, on ne vit qu'une fois.'

If any doubters still needed persuading that Adèle was the perfect soulmate for Johann, it was provided in the unlikeliest of places, the pages of the normally scathing and satirical publication, *Der Floh* ('The Flea'), which waxed positively lyrical:

> *Maestro Johann Strauss … needs a comfortable, gracious home, if he is to create with a joyful heart, if the refreshing spring of his lovely melodies is to flow unrestricted. Frau Adèle Strauss will offer him such a home. She will have a beneficial effect upon his nervous artistic temperament, and will be happy if she can give again to the honoured and beloved composer the peace of mind and happiness necessary for his creativity.*

This paean is all the remarkable, even prescient, for the fact that it was published on 25 March 1883. Given that Johann's divorce from Lili was granted on 9 December 1882, before which it would have been unthinkable for Adèle to move in with him, it must have been written at the most three months after the relationship became public. The effect of having Adèle living with him really *did* transform Johann Strauss.

But there was a problem, a huge problem. Johann and Adèle could not marry, as long as Lili lived. The divorce might have been granted by the civil authorities, but it was not accepted by the Roman Catholic Church in Austria to which Johann belonged. In fact Johann applied for papal consent to the divorce immediately after it was granted, but the Vatican refused.

There was another obstacle too. Adèle was Jewish. Under Austrian law, a Roman Catholic was forbidden to marry a Jew.[57]

In each case there was a solution, but it was drastic. Adèle did not hesitate: she gave up her Jewish faith and converted to Protestantism. As for Johann, well, then as now, there is no religious

---

[57] The irony of this was that Strauss himself had Jewish blood, as we shall see later.

Right

Poster for Johann
Strauss's *Wiener Blut*
waltz ('Viennese Blood').

law that cannot be bent with a little incentive mixed with a dose
of hypocrisy.

Twenty years previously Johann had dedicated a polka *'Neues
Leben'* ('New Life') to a member of the German aristocracy, Duke
Ernst II of Saxe-Coburg, himself an excellent musician and ama-
teur composer, perhaps better remembered as the elder brother of
Queen Victoria's consort, Prince Albert.

The duke, an admirer of Johann Strauss, was suitably flattered
and awarded him a decoration. If there was any debt still due to
Strauss, this was the moment he called it in. On 8 December 1885
Johann Strauss formally renounced his Austrian citizenship. Five
months later he applied to the City Magistrate of Coburg to become

a citizen of Coburg, pledging a donation to the local fund for the poor to oil the bureaucratic wheels.

On 24 June 1886 his new citizenship was confirmed, and two weeks later he officially left the Roman Catholic Church and became a Lutheran Protestant. In July the following year Duke Ernst used the powers invested in him to dissolve Strauss's marriage to Lili, and five weeks after that Johann and Adèle were married at the Coburg Register Office, with a religious service later that day in the ducal church.

The whole procedure had taken an inconveniently long time to come to fruition – almost two years from the time Johann first applied to relinquish his Austrian citizenship to the day he married Adèle – but come to fruition it had.

Johann Strauss was now married for the third time. And Johann Strauss, born in Vienna, whose music distilled the very essence of Vienna and the Viennese into musical notes, whose compositions were named for the Vienna woods, the Blue Danube, Viennese blood, even the city of Vienna itself, was now a German citizen!

❧

Johann Strauss had once again found happiness at home, but there was another area of his family life where relations were less pleasant, and this concerned his younger brother Eduard.

'Der schöne Edi' had not had an easy time of it. Rather like brother Josef he had not initially wanted a musical career, preferring to study for the diplomatic service. But again, as with Josef, his mother stepped in, decreeing that it was essential Eduard study music and enter the family firm. As I have already stated, she must have been overjoyed to find he did indeed possess musical talent. Once she knew that, there was no choice for Eduard but to join his brothers. He studied musical theory, as well as piano and violin. But here Johann intervened and pointed out that while there was no shortage of pianists and violinists, what was really needed was a harpist – they were much thinner on the ground. Johann, as well as being an established musician, was ten years older than Eduard, who therefore looked up to his brother in every respect.

Eduard studied the harp, but again like both his brothers he was soon composing as well as playing. In what can only be described as a quite extraordinary, I am sure unique, occurrence in any field of the arts, Eduard composed literally hundreds of pieces in his lifetime, as did Johann, Josef and indeed their father. Combine their compositions – and I am referring to works with opus numbers, in other words published music, as opposed to sketches – and it runs into thousands. Not even the Bach family can rival that.

If Johann was king of the waltz, and Josef a waltz master too, Eduard specialised in the quick polka. Of all his compositions, it is polkas such as *'Bahn frei!'* ('Clear the track!'), *'Mit Dampf'* ('Steam up'), *'Ausser Rand und Band'* ('Out of control'), *'Ohne Bremse'* ('Brakes off'), which have remained in the repertoire – the novelty and excitement of rail travel clearly exercising a great influence on him.

Eduard, as we have seen, was soon playing harp in his brother's orchestra, but it was as a conductor that Eduard Strauss truly made his name. Of his debut as conductor in 1862, at the age of twenty-seven, the Viennese periodical *Der Zwischenakt* commented:

> *Herr Strauss was enthusiastically greeted, and presented with rare feeling and accuracy all the waltzes composed by his brother Johann during this season. His conducting showed that in him we have a conductor of the same calibre. Long live the Strauss trinity!*

One can imagine the mixed emotions this must have caused in Eduard. On the one hand praise for his conducting abilities, but always in the shadow of his eldest brother.

By all accounts Eduard was something of a tyrant on the podium. He would accept nothing but the very best from his musicians, and he was not afraid to show who was in charge. When, in the spring of 1878, forty-one members of the orchestra refused to undertake a six-month tour of Germany and Sweden, Eduard unhesitatingly dismissed them.

He had a harsh tongue too. On receiving what he called a 'perfectly impudent' letter from the orchestra's principal cellist asking for a pay rise, he unleashed a four-page torrent of abuse, blatantly impugning the unfortunate cellist's musical talents: '… you dare to ask me for a salary increase? Must I remind you that there are twenty-three cello pieces here that *you are unable* to play?'

And one can imagine the tones in which he was accustomed to address his players, judging by a comment he made about the wind section in a letter to a friend: 'This instrument [the 'Flutophone'] is *supposed* to replace two flutes … Oh my dear honoured friend!

"Eduard would one day take revenge on his two brothers, after their deaths, in a devastating way."

Would that you could find an instrument that would replace *all wind players* …'

You have to conclude that Eduard Strauss, excellent conductor though he might have been, was not well liked by his musicians, and was certainly nowhere near as loved as his eldest brother.

What made matters worse for the players was that it was Eduard, not either of his brothers, who most often conducted them. Johann was averse to touring. When he did so, it was under protest. Josef had always resented standing in for his eldest brother and, following his untimely death, touring duties fell to the youngest, Eduard, who was equally resentful.

You can see why. Such was the universal popularity of the Johann Strauss Orchestra, it was in demand literally across the world. Eduard himself estimated later in life that in twenty-three years of touring with the Strauss Orchestra he visited 840 towns in two continents and gave concerts at 14 Exhibitions.

And therein lay the problem for Eduard. It was the *Strauss* Orchestra, and that meant only one thing for audiences. Even before Josef's death, although it was acknowledged in Vienna that there were three Strauss brothers, it was always a case of Johann – the eldest – and the other two. After Josef's death, Johann's pre-eminence was all the more assured.

Eduard had one eye on posterity, and there was only one way to ensure that as a musician: as composer not conductor. Here Johann's name was assured in perpetuity, such was the brilliance of his compositions, and Eduard was a good enough musician to know that as composer he simply was not in his elder brother's class.

We know of at least 300 published pieces by Eduard, but it would appear there could have been many more. Difficult though it might be to believe for a Strauss, Eduard was not always able to get his work published. Johann remarked in 1892: '[Edi's] compositions are not bad – but nobody wants to buy them.'

As a conductor, though, he was feted wherever he took the orchestra, nowhere more so and at a higher social level than in Britain. He played before Queen Victoria at both Windsor Castle and Buckingham Palace, as his father had done before him.

Above

A poster for Eduard Strauss's orchestra.

The queen, exhibiting either a formidable memory or an efficient briefing by her advisers, said to Eduard, 'You remind me very much of your father. It seems like only yesterday that he played at my Coronation Ball.' In fact it was fifty-six years earlier.

After a concert at Windsor Castle the queen presented him with a silver writing set, in the hope that he would use the pen in writing his next composition. In mentioning composition rather than conducting she will have pushed completely the right button. She certainly knew how to flatter him!

Eduard was himself equally adept at flattery. In his letter of thanks he described the evening at Windsor Castle as 'one of the most beautiful and memorable of my artistic career', adding, 'I and my family will always remember Her Majesty and the Royal Family with undying veneration.'

Johann was well aware that, because of his nightly appearances on the rostrum at Vienna's leading dance halls, Eduard was considerably better known in person than he was himself. Edi was frequently pictured and caricatured in the newspapers, with reviews describing his performances in detail. The epithet 'der schöne Edi' had well and truly stuck.

Despite the fact that Johann had, in effect, engineered this situation by avoiding performing, it appears his brother's popularity did occasionally get to him. There is anecdotal evidence that he would introduce himself by saying, 'I am Edi's brother.'

At times the tension between eldest and youngest brothers simmered over, and it seems it was usually Johann, playing the role of *paterfamilias*, who resorted to corrective action. In 1892, after what must have been close to a bust-up between them (we do not know the circumstances), Johann felt obliged to write to his brother:

You still see everything pessimistically – you always think that I am trying to score points over you. For goodness' sake, why won't you rid yourself of such foolish notions? How old do you have to become before you finally realise that your brother is not your enemy? … Sometimes our relationship has been worsened because of your sheer ambition, but you should know that my brotherly feelings towards you have never changed.

'*How old do you have to become … ?*' This admonishing note was written when Eduard was fifty-seven years of age!

Just how far relations between the two had deteriorated would become clear when Johann's will, written in 1895, omitted his brother entirely, on the grounds that 'he finds himself in favourable circumstances'.

It is true that Eduard earned a considerable amount of money as conductor of the Strauss Orchestra, not to mention a wide assortment of medals, decorations, medals of honour, golden snuffboxes, all the gifts a successful conductor can expect to have bestowed on him.

But Johann was not prepared to make changes to his will when, two years later, Eduard's financial position suddenly changed, and much for the worse. A codicil stated bluntly and unforgivingly:

Although the reasons for which I did not remember my dear brother Eduard in my will to my knowledge no longer apply, I will not make any alteration to take account of this. I hope that my brother's situation will improve.

So what accounted for Eduard's sudden reversal of fortune? Almost thirty-five years earlier, on 8 January 1863, Eduard had married Maria Magdalena Klenkhart, the youngest daughter of a coffee house owner who had been a friend of Johann Strauss the elder.

The couple had two sons, interestingly named Johann and Josef (one suspects Anna's controlling hand in this). We owe a debt of gratitude to Johann for carrying the Strauss musical tradition into the next century. But the two sons, in connivance with their mother, would later spend every penny of their father's hard-earned fortune, leaving him destitute.

As for Eduard himself, he would one day take revenge on his two brothers, after their deaths, in a devastating way, the consequences of which we are still suffering today.

Chapter Sixteen
TRAGEDY IN THE IMPERIAL ROYAL FAMILY

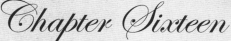

*T*he year is **1888** and Franz Josef has been Emperor of Austria for forty years. He is fifty-eight years of age, and already to his people he is 'the old emperor'. He has a kindly, avuncular face, a half-smile always present, eyes slightly closed, causing friendly wrinkles to emanate from their corners. He is universally respected, even if 'loved' is a touch too strong a word for a man who rules through divine providence.

Those who had predicted he would soon relinquish the throne after being placed there in fraught circumstances in 1848 had been long since proved mistaken. In fact he had won the affection and admiration of his people on that day in February 1853 when he had survived an assassination attempt. Where had he been at the time, and what had he been doing? Was he fulfilling some official function, surrounded by advisers and soldiers? No, he had been strolling with one of his officers, a good friend, on the Bastei, mingling easily with other Viennese following the same pursuit.

The high, sturdy collar of his military uniform had saved his life. What no one could have known at the time is that what, if the assassination attempt had succeeded, would have been a brief five-year reign, forgotten to history, was to become a reign lasting sixty-eight years, almost the longest to this day in European history.

But as the Viennese prepared to put on a show for Franz Josef's fortieth jubilee celebrations, neither for them nor their emperor had it been four decades of trouble-free existence.

In the first place the fairytale marriage of the young emperor to the young and beautiful Duchess Elisabeth of Bavaria, known as Sisi, had turned out to be anything but. From the day she arrived by boat in Vienna, Sisi had hated the formality and protocol of the imperial

court. She did not get on with her domineering mother-in-law, and longed for the freedom of her childhood home, Possenhofen Castle, on the shore of Lake Starnberg in Bavaria.

Sisi was not one to bow to convention, however lofty. She had a mind of her own. She shocked her mother-in-law by having a gym installed in her apartment in the Hofburg Palace; she frequently indulged her passion for horses and riding; she insisted on preserving and exhibiting her beauty by combing her lustrous hair into which she set jewels, and having her ladies-in-waiting tie her into almost

Above

The assassination attempt on Emperor Franz Josef, shortly after he came to the throne.

Right

Empress Elisabeth
liked to flatter her very
narrow waist with belts
pulled tight.

impossibly small-waisted dresses.[58] It was behaviour that bordered
on the eccentric; certainly not to be expected of an empress.

She adhered to a strict diet. Meat disgusted her, so that a meal
might consist of the juice of half-raw beef squeezed into thin soup,

---

[58] Known as 'tight-lacing'.

or a diet of just milk and eggs. She ate small amounts and very quickly, as if trying to avoid any long-term effect on her weight. If the smallness of her waist was in any way threatened, she would fast completely for several days. Today we would not hesitate to say she suffered from an eating disorder.

There is no question that her mental health was fragile, both genetically – there was inbreeding to the extent that her mother-in-law was also her aunt – and as an independent retaliation against a world she wished every minute of the day and night she had never joined.[59]

After her first child, Sophie, died at the age of just two, she refused to eat for days. As with Sophie, a second daughter was immediately taken away from her. Her mother-in-law refused to allow her to breastfeed or to have anything to do with the baby's care. Such treatment worsened her already erratic behaviour, leading to bouts of depression that consumed her for weeks.

Her husband, by contrast, was a simple soldier – his own description – with all a soldier's instincts for discipline, obedience, an acceptance of duty and obligation. He was ill-equipped mentally to deal with a highly strung woman whose beauty was legendary throughout Europe, who made her own decisions about how and where to spend her time, and with whom.

Franz Josef indulged his wife in every way that he was capable of. When she developed a passion for Greece, he had a palace built for her on the island of Corfu. She rarely visited it.[60] When she announced that she was travelling to Britain and Ireland to go riding to hounds, he allowed it – refusing to listen to rumours that she was having an affair with the dashing Scottish horseman, Bay Middleton.

The Viennese, who had really wanted to love their empress, had long since realised that was an impossible wish. If anything, Elisabeth's eccentricities, which made life so difficult for her husband, increased the people's affection, even sympathy, for their emperor.

---

[59] In fact she had not been intended as the emperor's bride. His mother had chosen Elisabeth's elder sister, but Josef fell in love with Elisabeth and proposed to her.

[60] Today it is a museum to Empress Elisabeth owned by the Greek nation.

Archduke Rudolf
lying in state, a wide
bandage concealing
the fatal gunshot
wound to the head.

Empress Elisabeth visited her son and kissed his lips. Her younger daughter, Archduchess Marie Valerie (known as Valerie), who accompanied her, gave an account of the scene, at the same time leaving us a witheringly accurate description of her brother's character:

He was so handsome and lay there so peacefully, the white sheet pulled up to his chest and flowers strewn all around. The narrow [sic] bandage on his head did not disfigure him – his cheeks and ears were still rosy with the healthy glow of youth – the restless, often bitter, scornful expression that was often characteristic of him in life had given way to a perfect smile. He never seemed so beautiful to me before – he seemed to be asleep and calm, happy.

Hardly surprisingly the sudden death – and its manner – of the heir to the throne, and of a son who rarely saw his mother and did not get on with his father, did nothing to bring his parents any closer together.

It was Empress Elisabeth who was told the news first, initially complaining that she had given instructions that her daily Greek lesson should never be interrupted. She then told her husband.

Significantly she did not attend Rudolf's funeral, preferring to remain in prayer in a private chapel.

Also unsurprising, given what we know of their characters, is the different way in which each parent reacted to Rudolf's death. As a father Franz Josef grieved for his son, but the military bearing and discipline never wavered, at least in public. 'I bore up well,' he said after the funeral. 'It was only in the crypt that I could endure it no longer.'

There is no question that uppermost in his mind was the fact the heir to the Habsburg throne was now dead. What would that mean for the empire? Would it in any way weaken it? Would its enemies try to capitalise on the grave situation?

As for Elisabeth, she was riven with guilt. Not, it seems, for the fact she more or less deserted her son and had taken little interest in his upbringing or welfare, but for fear that she had passed on her family's mental instability – madness, not to put too fine a point on it – to her son.

If she believed what the Roman Catholic Church said, she had good reason to feel guilty. Like the Cistercian abbot, the pope himself had proved remarkably susceptible to inducements of one kind or another, finally allowing himself to be persuaded that Rudolf's suicide was not your normal suicide, but the consequence of 'a state of mental derangement', thus allowing Rudolf complete burial rites.

Rudolf thus suffered officially from mental derangement, and why might that be? His mother believed for the rest of her life that she at least bore some responsibility for that dreadful act on the night of 30 January 1889.

Rudolf's coffin took its place in the Imperial Crypt in the Augustinerkirche in the Neuer Markt in the centre of Vienna, where it would later be joined by those of his parents. They lie alongside each other to this day, closer in death than they ever were in life.

❦

Vienna was in a state of shock. No living Viennese had known of such a portentous act. The nineteenth century had certainly been one of upheavals, and you only had to be in late middle age to have witnessed the street revolution of 1848 and the ignominious middle-of-the-night departure of the politician who had ruled with an iron fist, Klemens von Metternich.

There had already been one death in the imperial royal family. The emperor's brother, Archduke Maximilian, who had been installed on the throne of faraway Mexico, had been executed by firing squad in June 1867.[64]

There had been wars, both victories and defeats, even an economic crash. But of one thing it was possible to be absolutely sure: the Habsburg dynasty, secure for six hundred years, was immutable. An emperor died or abdicated, and his legitimate and rightful heir would succeed. This progression had come to a sudden and unnatural stop.

What no one could know, not the emperor himself nor his wife, was that the killing was not yet over. Another single and unnatural death would haunt Vienna, and the empire, within a few short years. And that in turn would be followed by more killing, on a hitherto unimaginable scale. It would run into millions.

But that lay ahead. For now, the people of Vienna who had celebrated the emperor's fortieth anniversary with such *élan*, found themselves thrown into the deepest mourning. And who, once again, did they turn to when in need of gaiety and laughter?

Why, the Waltz King, of course.

---

[64] He had done his duty, said the emperor, ever the military man.

Chapter Seventeen
THE 'EMPEROR WALTZ'

There are **numerous** photographs of Emperor Franz Josef, at least from middle age onwards, and dozens of painted portraits, facsimiles of which still hang in many a government office or hotel reception room today. They show the kindly visage, worn down by tragedy and the relentless unpredictability of events – 'Gentlemen, my hand is unlucky,' he once said to city officials, and that was before the final tragedy – but if you want a true character study of this longest serving of monarchs, *Der alte Herr* ('the Old Gentleman') to the people of his day and a century of succeeding generations, you need look no further than Johann Strauss the Younger.

In the autumn of 1889, the year following the fortieth jubilee of the emperor's reign, Strauss composed a new waltz entitled *'Hand in Hand'*. It was one of the pieces he intended performing in Berlin at a week of concerts, and the title was meant to echo a recent toast of friendship that Franz Josef had made to the German kaiser.

However, Strauss's Berlin publisher, Fritz Simrock[65] had the rather good idea that the piece should be renamed *'Kaiser-Walzer'* ('Emperor Waltz'), a title that could refer to either monarch, and thus be suitably flattering to both. He went ahead with his plan, published the piece under the new title, and thereby gave the world a single piece of music that many consider to be the finest, and at the same time most poignant, that Strauss ever composed.

---

[65] Grandson of Nikolaus Simrock, friend of Beethoven in Bonn, and founder of the music-publishing house that bears his name.

The Swiss music critic William Ritter described the *'Emperor Waltz'* as symphonic, more tone-poem than dance, and 'the most beautiful flower the fantastic tree of Strauss's music has borne'.

The German dramatist and novelist Paul Lindau wrote to Strauss:

> *It is no exaggeration when I say that, in my musical view, nothing has been written since the days of Franz Schubert which, for pure melody and unspoiled beauty, can be compared with the first part of your* 'Kaiser-Walzer'. *In those [opening] bars there is more music, genuine, unadulterated music, than in many operas that last a whole evening but which leave the heart empty.*

There certainly is. The opening is in fact a slow march. What is a march? Something boisterous, loud, noisy, to stamp booted feet to.

Strauss's first stroke of genius is to mark the opening bars *pianissimo*, as quiet as possible. The effect is to make you lean forward, strain your ears, to catch what is being played.

These opening bars capture instantly the character of Emperor Franz Josef. He is a military man, but a quiet one. Not a soldier to stamp and shout, but one who quietly gives orders and is prepared to obey them with total discipline when required.

The German-born journalist and writer Heinrich Eduard Jacob, author of *Johann Strauss: A Century of Light Music*, described this opening passage as 'very discreet, which is not typical of Strauss', and adds:

> *Strauss possibly wrote nothing more beautiful – and nothing less like the Strauss as Vienna's dance enthusiasts conceived him – than this march, which excites by its very tranquillity.*

Strauss then lifts the volume slightly to *piano*, gives a foretaste of the beautiful waltz to come, then increases the volume more and more to a *forte*, bringing the entire orchestra in for a full-blown march.

But this does not last. It is as if the emperor himself is saying, 'No no, this is too public, too indiscreet, we must maintain our royal dignity.' A lone cello comes in, high in the upper register, with a theme so plaintive the emperor himself could be shedding tears.

With just solo cello sounding, the time changes to three-four, Strauss writes *Tempo di Valse* at the top of the score, and gives us the most heartrendingly beautiful waltz, with plunging intervals of an octave, a seventh, even a ninth. It is the sound, almost, of a sob, but as with everything about his subject, a controlled sob.

But why just one waltz, when two will do? And what a contrast the second waltz is. High violins and flute take the theme, with horns and oboe in counterpoint. This is the emperor remembering better days, when he was young and taking as his bride the most beautiful young duchess in Europe.

Memories, though, are painful for Franz Josef. A waltz like this cannot endure, and again it is high violins and flute that drift down, a melancholy phrase that does not so much end as peter out, as the first waltz comes back in, and we are once again in the emperor's private world, and once again *pianissimo*.

Back comes the second waltz, but still *pianissimo*, as though, try as he might, there can be no relief from the melancholia that sits on Franz Josef's shoulders. A brief passage played *fortissimo*, allowing him temporary respite, gives way to a new waltz, a descending phrase once more filled with sadness. At intervals musical laughter breaks out, but each time it is quickly stifled.

A third waltz now, and it is joyous. No matter what befalls him, Franz Josef refuses to surrender totally to despair. And back comes the march. The emperor on parade, inspecting his troops, relishing their respectful and admiring gaze.

And we are into yet a fourth waltz, pointed and even piquant, as Franz Josef enjoys a little humour with staff officers. But once again it is not allowed to last, as the very first waltz returns in an inverted version. Instead of the theme plunging huge intervals, it rises. But Strauss keeps hold of the reins, not allowing the sound to rise above *mezzo forte*.

Soon we are back into melancholia, and the first waltz with those plunging intervals, the controlled sobs once more, with the sound not rising above *piano*. Is the emperor wiping away tears as news reaches him of the tragedy at Mayerling?

Life must go on. A soldier's discipline will ensure he does not surrender. The march returns, as Franz Josef gratefully receives the enhanced love of his people, who want to share his pain at the loss of his son, their future emperor, in order to alleviate it if they possibly can.

Through the sadness of the first waltz, the emperor is determined to show his people that they have helped him come through the worst of times. Trombones and trumpets sound the martial notes that allow him to bestride the parade ground, his palace, the duties of state.

But he knows, they know, that in the end he will be overwhelmed by fate, by forces he cannot control. The march is abruptly cut off, and the lone voice of the cello returns, like a Cassandra with nothing to impart but prophecies of more tragedy to come.

And in the face of such predictions, the emperor behaves like any soldier – with defiance and dignity, a refusal to be cowed. So the music builds finally to a *fortissimo* finish. Nothing will break this man.

If I have taken a certain artistic licence in my descriptive analysis of the *'Emperor Waltz'*, one factor in Johann Strauss's life most certainly supports it. He knew the emperor well, and even if his intention had not been to create a portrait in music of the man, he must have realised how apt it was. Why else would he have agreed to the title being changed?

His role as Court Ball Director of Music brought him into frequent contact with the emperor and empress, even though they were hardly great concertgoers or aficionados of music. He was required to compose new pieces for special state occasions. For the emperor's diamond jubilee he composed the *'Kaiser-Jubiläum Jubelwalzer'* ('Jubilee Waltz for the Emperor's Jubilee'), which became instantly popular, even if it was to be rather eclipsed by the *'Emperor Waltz'*, which followed a year later.[66]

It seems Johann Strauss knew the emperor on another level as well. The emperor's mistress, Katharina Schratt – Kathi to those close to her – was now fully accepted as part of his life. Should there be any doubt, the empress herself made a point of being seen both at court and in public together with her husband and Kathi, an overt declaration of her approval for what amounted to a *ménage à trois*.

For Kathi actually to take up residence in either the Hofburg or Schönbrunn Palace, though, would be considered a step too far, and so the emperor bought a villa for her in the Gloriettegasse, a secluded tree-lined street just outside the garden walls of Schönbrunn in Hietzing. Kathi was therefore on hand whenever the emperor was able to escape from his official residence in the centre of Vienna to the beautiful summer palace in Hietzing.

The wealthy suburb of Hietzing had both good, and not so good, memories for Strauss. It was where Dommayer's Casino stood, the

---

[66] In fact several Strauss biographies mistakenly state that the *'Emperor Waltz'* was specifically composed for the Jubilee.

venue that had seen his debut as conductor and composer nearly half a century earlier. It was also where he had lived contentedly with the wife he adored, Jetty, and where she had died.

We do not know under exactly what circumstances, but residents of Hietzing, well into the next century, spoke excitedly of the famous personages who frequented their district. It was said that the emperor himself would walk out of Schönbrunn Palace early of a summer's morning, stroll across to Kathi's villa, let himself in through the garden gate, and join his mistress for breakfast.

Johann Strauss, the locals said, often joined them, albeit later in the day. And do you know what the great composer liked to eat, they'd ask? Crayfish and goose-liver pâté, served with very dry champagne. Kathi always made sure she had it available to serve to him.

It's impossible to know exactly how much of this is true, though stories like that are usually founded on at least a modicum of truth. In fact only one conversation between Strauss and the emperor is actually authenticated, because it was witnessed by a number of people.

It took place on a glittering occasion. In 1894 Vienna celebrated the golden jubilee of Johann Strauss's career as a musician. It was fifty years since, as a nervous and apprehensive young man, he had stood in front of his orchestra at Dommayer's Casino, expressly against his father's wishes, and performed his first public concert.

Now, in his seventieth year, he was the object of veneration and admiration. A week of festivities was held in the city he had portrayed so many times in music, and the Viennese people, from lowest to highest, joined in the celebrations. The highest being the emperor himself.

The high point of the celebrations was a gala performance of Strauss's operetta *Der Zigeunerbaron*. To the surprise of the sophisticated audience in the Vienna State Opera, and to their delight, the emperor himself took his seat in the royal box.

Visits to the opera not being a regular feature of the emperor's duties, on the rare occasions when he did attend he would slip discreetly away during the second act. Since it was customary for the composer, or noted actor or singer (as with Katharina Schratt) to be presented to the emperor, this would happen during the first intermission, since by the end of the performance he would no longer be there.

Right
The elegant Café
Zauner in Bad Ischl,
frequented by Brahms
and the emperor's
mistress, Kathi Schratt.

On it Brahms wrote, 'Service at the Court of Adèle' and beneath it, 'Brahms for fugues, Strauss for waltzes.'

On another occasion Adèle spotted Brahms in a restaurant. She went over to him and asked if he would sign a napkin for her. He took a pen, wrote out the opening bars of the *'Blue Danube'* waltz, and signed underneath, 'Alas not by Johannes Brahms' (*Leider nicht von Johannes Brahms*).[67]

Brahms was no mere flatterer when it came to his praise of Strauss's music. He would frequently sit at the piano and play the waltzes. The Hungarian composer Karl Goldmark once witnessed Brahms play the whole of *'By the Beautiful Blue Danube'* on the piano. He described how Brahms played an improvisation of the introduction, and then proceeded to produce a 'marvel of spontaneous evolution of the musical material'.

Both Strauss and Brahms had a favourite destination that they would go to in the summer to get away from the oppressive heat of Vienna – Strauss on the advice of his doctor to counter bouts of illness. It was the beautiful spa town of Bad Ischl, some 170 miles

---

[67] Other versions of this famous anecdote have Brahms signing Adèle's fan, or a score of *'By the Beautiful Blue Danube'*.

south-west of Vienna, on the edge of the Salzkammergut mountain range, which stretches east from Salzburg across Upper Austria.

Both men had villas on the same slope leading up from the crystal-clear waters of the River Traun.[68] On the other side of Bad Ischl, on a wooded rise, was the grand summer palace given to young Franz Josef as a wedding present from his mother. He loved to spend time there, describing it as 'heaven on earth'. Sisi rarely, if ever, went there – it held too many bad memories. In her eyes it represented the beginning of her 'enslavement' as a member of the imperial royal family.

The palace was conveniently placed for the emperor. A short walk along the river, through a gate, and he was inside a villa that his mistress Kathi Schratt had acquired. The convenience was mutual. Kathi was given a key to the emperor's villa – by Sisi herself. A photograph taken in 1910, when the emperor was eighty years of age and Kathi approaching fifty-seven, shows them walking as a couple in the grounds of the imperial villa in Bad Ischl.

The emperor, in dark military uniform with resplendent whiskers, looks weighed down by matters of state. His mistress, in smart suit, fur stole round her shoulders, stylish hat, parasol in right hand, is talking to him. It looks as though she, a retired actress who left her youth and looks long behind, is counselling him, offering advice to this man who had ruled his empire for more than sixty years. Not for nothing was she known as 'the uncrowned Empress of Austria'.[69]

Johannes Brahms and Johann Strauss spent many a summer month in Bad Ischl, often planning their visits so they would be there at the same time. It is not known whether either of the composers met the emperor in Ischl, though it seems more than likely. What is known is that towards the end of his life, Brahms would stroll to the elegant Café Zauner to join Kathi Schratt for tea and pastries.

Strauss delighted in playing ideas to Brahms on the piano, and they chatted and drank for many an hour. Proof of just how comfortable these two great musicians, two such different individuals,

> *"Brahms's works were deep, even dense, intended to engage the mind. Johann Strauss, by contrast, was a showman."*

---

[68] The house Brahms rented is still there. On the site where Strauss's villa stood there is now an unprepossessing modern apartment block.

[69] See chapter 21, page 241.

Right

Strauss standing on
the veranda of his villa
with Johannes Brahms,
two great composers
who enjoyed each
other's company. One
is nearly a decade older
than the other.

were in each other's company is another photograph, this one earlier than that showing Franz Josef and Kathi, taken in September 1894.

It shows Strauss and Brahms standing on the veranda of Strauss's villa. Brahms, on the right, has receding grey hair exposing a high domed forehead and a full snowy white beard falling to his chest. He is heavily built – grossly overweight in today's terms.

His all-black suit is shapeless. His black shoes are dull and unpolished. The only concession to anything not black is a gold or silver watch chain. His left arm is stretched onto the balcony balustrade, causing his jacket – already several sizes too long, reaching almost to his knees – to fall open and appear several sizes too big.

What a contrast Johann Strauss provides! Dark dyed-black hair swept luxuriantly back, neatly trimmed black moustache, his clothes looking as if they might have come straight off a showroom mannequin. Stylish dark jacket, immaculately creased black-and-white-checked trousers, dark waistcoat, white winged-collar shirt with flamboyantly knotted silver tie, shoes polished like mirrors.

He has a trim figure, with not an ounce of spare flesh on him. His left arm is also on the balcony balustrade, but casually bent at the elbow, matching the left leg seductively bent at the knee.

Neither man is smiling, but I am ready to bet that if Strauss's upper lip were not entirely hidden by his moustache, it would reveal a suppressed smile.

As with Strauss and the emperor, if you were challenged to put an age to each man, you could quite easily say that Brahms was around seventy years of age, whereas Strauss might be somewhere around fifty, quite possibly even in his late forties.

When the photograph was taken, Johannes Brahms was sixty-one years and four months, whereas Johann Strauss was just one month short of his seventieth birthday!

Another photograph taken the following year shows Strauss at work on the same veranda of his house in Bad Ischl. There is the tall desk that he liked to stand at to compose, which befitted his restless nature. Manuscript papers are on the desktop, a pen is in his right hand. The forearm of his bent left arm rests on the desktop. This time the anxious look is back on his face.[70]

---

[70] See chapter 12, page 125.

The picture is totally posed. One can almost hear the photographer telling him to try to relax, to bend the left knee, rest the left arm on the desktop. Equally I am sure Strauss is muttering under his breath, 'Just hurry up and be done with it. I have work to do.'

Johann Strauss at work was a very different individual from the man relaxing with his good friend Johannes Brahms.

Despite his youthful appearance, age was taking its toll on Johann Strauss. Always with an edgy, difficult side to his character, now as he approached seventy he had no need to hide or curb it. He was world famous; his compositions were adored across continents. He hobnobbed with royalty. If he wanted to be difficult, unsociable, who was to tell him not to be? Most certainly not his wife, who was more than content to indulge her famous husband.

If this side to his character was now exhibited in public, what did it matter? He could survive anything that his detractors might say against him. And some of them had very harsh things indeed to say.

The Viennese newspaper *Die Presse*, unimpressed with the elaborate celebrations of Strauss's golden jubilee, made its views known in unrestrained language:

> *Strauss is nervy and a hypochondriac. He has every possible and impossible illness, especially suffering from the same malady as some acquaintance who has just died. In actual fact, there is nothing wrong with him. But one is never quite as ill as when one is suffering from an illness one doesn't have.*

Die Presse was at least partly right. Strauss was a hypochondriac, and always had been. His brother Josef had practically accused him to his face of feigning illness during his trips to Russia all those years ago.

But as old age crept over him, there is no doubt that his health did actually suffer. Always with the caveat that any kind of retrospective diagnosis more than one and a quarter centuries after the event is fraught with danger, a doctor today might well find on examining him that Strauss suffered from neuralgia, arthritis, chronic bronchitis and influenza.

But there was quite possibly more to it than physical ailments. Beginning in 1983 the Austrian musicologist and Strauss specialist,

Professor Franz Mailer, published ten annotated volumes of Strauss family letters and documents over almost thirty years. He wrote, 'Many signs lead one to infer [that Johann Strauss suffered from] severe psychiatric illness.'

Contemporary accounts are similar. The author Ignaz Schnitzer, who wrote the libretto for *Der Zigeunerbaron* and therefore worked closely with Strauss, relates how Strauss's mood could suddenly, and dangerously, change:

> *Morose, unspeaking, hardly looking up, he would skulk for days or weeks on end unsociably around the house, or keep himself cocooned in his work room. His own wife hardly dared to speak to him then, since to be disturbed in this ill-humoured silence could bring him to furious agitation.*

In the last decade of his life Strauss would spend the summers in Bad Ischl, the winters at his house in the Igelgasse. While he enjoyed the warm scented air in the Salzkammergut, in the city during winter he would complain of pain and tiredness and more or less confine himself to his room.

Both in Bad Ischl and Vienna he continued his habit of composing mostly at night, as he had told the American journalist in New York many years before. Beside his work desk in the Igelgasse house was a bell, which he rang to summon Adèle at any hour of the night to hear a new tune he had created.

Inevitably his nocturnal habits affected his eyesight, and increased his overall melancholy. In October 1894, just days after his golden-jubilee celebrations, he wrote to his brother Eduard:

> *I see everything double. If I take a toothpick, I always see two before me. If I should have the misfortune to go blind, I shall shoot myself. Of all physical ailments, this is the most insurmountable. Not to read – [or] be able to write, would take away from me all joy of life.*

Alongside Johann's obsessive fear of death, he also developed a phobia of disease and avoided anything that could bring him into contact with it. One of these possible sources of illness was Adèle's daughter Alice. Johann adored her as if she were his own child, but he strictly forbade her to invite her friends into his house for fear of catching some childhood ailment from them.

Of one fact Johann Strauss was acutely aware, and it was unique to him among composers. Strauss owed more to the city of his birth,

> *"Alongside Johann's obsessive fear of death, he also developed a phobia of disease and avoided anything that could bring him into contact with it."*

Vienna, than he could ever repay. No great composer of the nineteenth century had rooted his music so firmly in the city of his birth.

As I have already noted, only one other truly great musical name of the nineteenth century was actually born in Vienna, as opposed to moving to live there, and that was Franz Schubert. Describe Schubert's music in any way you wish, but to call it typically Viennese would be wrong. It is typically Schubertian.

Strauss's music alone distils the essence of Vienna into musical notes, and he knew it. At the festival banquet held at the Grand Hotel in Vienna for his golden jubilee, in the company of two hundred people, including composers, writers and artists, he responded to a toast in his honour with these words:

> *If it is true that I have some talent, then I have to thank for its development my dear native city of Vienna, in whose earth my whole strength is rooted, in whose air lie the sounds which my ear gathers, which my heart takes in and my hand writes down … Vienna, the heart of our beautiful, God-blessed Austria … to her I give my cheer: Vienna, bloom, prosper and grow!*

Vienna was not to obey his command. The city, the country, the empire, was heading inexorably towards oblivion. Johann Strauss would not live to witness that. But he would live to see the next great personal tragedy unfold, a tragedy so profound and unexpected that Emperor Franz Josef, on being informed, would visibly shrink and age.

'Am I then to be spared nothing?' the emperor would ask, trying with all the military discipline he could muster to contain his grief.

Chapter Eighteen

An Assassin's Knife Breaks the Emperor's Heart

Dixième année. — N° 503.　　Huit pages : CINQ centimes　　Dimanche 25 Septembre. 1898.

Le Petit Parisien

SUPPLÉMENT LITTÉRAIRE ILLUSTRÉ

TOUS LES JOURS
Petit Parisien
5 CENTIMES.

DIRECTION: 18, rue d'Enghien, PARIS

TOUS LES JEUDIS
SUPPLÉMENT LITTÉRAIRE
5 CENTIMES.

L'ASSASSINAT DE L'IMPÉRATRICE D'AUTRICHE

Le Quai du Mont-Blanc, à Genève
Où Luccheni a commis l'assassinat

PORTRAIT DE LUCCHENI

La Villa Achilléion, à Corfou
Où l'Impératrice avait demandé à être inhumée

*I*n one of those quirks of history, two men whose names were previously unknown would soon enter the story of the Habsburg empire. The second of these, whom I will address later, would fire a volley of shots that would kill two people, and lead to the deaths of millions. The first would wield a stiletto knife, kill a single person, and bring a man already tortured with pain and regret to unknown despair.

The name Luigi Luccheni is forgotten to history, but for a brief moment in September 1898 it was emblazoned across the newspapers of the world. Born in Paris to Italian parents, he grew up as an orphan, working later as labourer and bricklayer, then as a cavalry officer's servant. At some stage in young adulthood he became an anarchist, joined the extremist 'Regicide Squad', and set himself the task, or was assigned the task by colleagues, of assassinating a member of European royalty, a 'great deed' from which the monarchies of Europe would not recover. The chosen target was Prince Henri of Orléans, pretender to the throne of France. The prince was known to be intending to visit Geneva, and so Luccheni based himself there.

Several hundred miles north of Geneva, in central Germany, the Empress of Austria was in the spa town of Bad Nauheim enjoying a rest and buying presents for her grandchildren. Actually, 'enjoying' is not entirely the right word. Her daughter Archduchess Marie Valerie, who had been with her for two weeks in Bad Ischl, described her as being 'in low spirits, as always'. Bad Ischl had that effect on her.

Valerie sided with her mother and largely blamed the emperor for 'the melancholic effect of court life, this exclusion from all natural

I have my hands full with the ballet. I am writing my fingers to the bone, and still make no headway. I am on the 40th sheet (full score) and have only managed 2 scenes.

By late autumn Johann had completed the first draft of the ballet, which was called *Aschenbrödel* ('Cinderella'). He interrupted work on it to conduct just the overture at a special matinee performance of *Die Fledermaus* at the Vienna Court Opera House on 22 May 1899, to mark the traditional springtime holiday.

Why only the overture, as opposed to the whole work? All his life Johann had been ambivalent towards conducting. First Josef, then Eduard, had taken on the conducting while he got on with composition – to him a much more worthwhile pursuit.

This gives the lie to the thousands of images and statuettes we have today of Johann Strauss, violin in one hand, bow raised high in the other, one hip cocked, one knee bent, a trance-like smile of happiness etched on his face as he leads his orchestra. It might be an exaggeration to say he hated directing the orchestra, and more truthful to say he did it because he knew he had to. When, sometime in late middle age, he began to suffer from arthritis and could no longer play the violin, he happily swapped it for the baton. He would just as happily have given that up too.

A letter he wrote to Eduard made it clear that it was his health, once again, that was dictating his musical career:

On account of my health I must, as much as possible, keep away from conducting ... because at the end of a number I leave the orchestra as if bathed in sweat, and unlike another person I cannot simply change my underclothes. I have to stay in the same attire for 5–6 hours, until the soaked outfit dries out by itself.

His compromise, in later years, was to agree to conduct the overture alone then hand the baton to a conductor who would take over for the rest of the performance. As far as we know, the last time Johann conducted an entire operetta was the 200th performance of *Die Fledermaus* at the Theater an der Wien on 15 May 1888.

Now, eleven years later almost to the day, he agreed to conduct the overture to his most popular and beloved work at the Vienna Court Opera House. It was not only to be the last time he would conduct, but the last time he would appear in public.

Chapter Nineteen
A FINAL *FLEDERMAUS*
AND JOHANN STRAUSS BIDS FAREWELL

Those who were there said Johann Strauss conducted the overture to *Die Fledermaus* with a vigour and intensity they had not seen before, as if somehow he knew it would be the last time.

They were, of course, speaking with the benefit of hindsight. But I imagine the eyes blazing, sweat already breaking out on his forehead in nervous anticipation, perhaps a last run of the left hand through the hair, before bringing the baton down for the rising notes that begin the orchestral swell.

A brisk twelve-bar introduction of runs and triplets that come to rest in a single held note. Some soft *staccato* chords and an oboe soars above. The violins take over, there's a long *crescendo*, and then *fortissimo* the violins rise, syncopated chords, and we are into the first theme taken from the operetta itself, into a second theme, and already the audience is swaying to melodies that are so well known, not just across Vienna and Europe, but the world.

What is going through Johann's mind? Is he asking himself why he was never able to repeat the success of this, his best-loved operetta? He has little time to contemplate, as *staccato pianissimo* notes in violins and cellos lead without a pause straight into the first waltz, which with its turning phrase and firm end notes seems to distil the essence of Vienna, a tune beloved of whistling *fiacre* drivers, as they gently gird their decorated horses into a trot.

The waltz repeats itself, this time *forte* for good measure, before leading straight into a second waltz, which springs high to the top of the E string for the first violins. And yet a third waltz, to which the audience hums along, smiling at the familiarity.

A march then, to which the characters will soon be stomping across the stage. We are already at Prince Orlofsky's ball, where all the masked chicanery will take place. But this is the overture. It must offer contrast, and so Strauss pulls it back, to a *piano* repeat of the opening. Mustn't give too much of the plot away yet.

And back comes the great opening waltz, again that stroke of genius to have it played *pianissimo*, make the audience strain forward to be sure they can catch it. Then give it to them full, *forte*.

The second waltz returns, now *fortissimo*, with high leaps once again in the first violins. Back comes the march, *piano*, then strings and wind in unison as the pace quickens. Notes fly off into the air, *fortissimo* now, and a sequence of unison chords tells us the overture is about to reach its climax – and end.

contributed to the world by his creations, Johann Strauss would be regard-
ed as one of the greatest benefactors of the century.

Some years ago I interviewed the president and first violinist of the Vienna Philharmonic Orchestra, Dr Clemens Hellsberg, for a radio programme I was making entitled *Vienna, City of Music*.

We stood in the aisle of the Golden Hall of the Musikverein, gilded statues looking down on us. Dr Hellsberg pointed to the spot above the stage on the left where Johannes Brahms sat and heard a performance of his Fourth Symphony, just a month before he died.

We spoke of Bruckner and Wagner, Mahler and Richard Strauss. Finally I asked him a question I was determined to ask, but hesitated to do so in case he dismissed it with a wave of the hand, as if to say, 'We are talking of *serious* music here.'

I asked, 'Here we are in Vienna, in the famous concert hall where the New Year's Day concert takes place every year, and where the *"Blue Danube Waltz"* is heard each time. What is it about the music of Johann Strauss, do you think, that makes it so enduring and so universally loved?'

A smile instantly settled on his face, much to my relief. He thought for just a brief moment, and then said, 'Strauss makes you happy.'

There was one notable absentee from Johann Strauss's funeral: his brother Eduard. Life had not been kind to the youngest of the Strauss brothers. He was now sixty-four and a man with problems.

He was also a man with a plan. It was an extraordinary plan, to us an inexplicable one. He would soon commit the single worst act of vandalism in the history of music.

Chapter Twenty

EDUARD'S FLAMES
OF REVENGE

It seems difficult, if not impossible, for us today to know exactly how or why the money was squandered. I have been unable to unearth any details; it is quite possible Eduard never revealed what was behind it, or even destroyed the evidence. All we know is that after he discovered the loss, Eduard went to his elder brother for financial help, and was refused.

The affair ended Eduard's marriage. He separated from his wife Maria, and became largely estranged from his two sons.

All of which meant that if Eduard was dreaming of a comfortable retirement, he needed to think again. In the autumn of 1899, at the age of sixty-four, and just months after the death of Johann (by which time we can assume he knew from Johann's will that he was to receive nothing), he signed a contract for yet another intensive tour.

He was off to North America again, almost a decade after the last tour. In a period of just under four months, spanning the turn of the century, he gave daily concerts and matinées twice a week, a total of 106 concerts, in seventy-three different places.

Now in his mid-sixties, Eduard paid the price for his exacting itinerary. In New Orleans, Chicago and San Francisco he had to be treated for malaria, while in Montreal it was problems of a different nature. The large French-speaking community was angry that advertisements for the concerts were placed only in the English-language newspapers, and so boycotted the concerts.

Troubles for Eduard and his orchestra did not end there. In the early morning of 7 February 1901, with just five engagements left, the train they were travelling on was involved in a collision as it pulled into Pittsburgh. Eduard dislocated his right shoulder.

For the remaining concerts, which culminated in a benefit ball in New York, Eduard was forced to conduct with his left arm, no doubt in considerable pain from the dislocation. At the end of the ball he knew he was laying down his baton for the last time. Did it make him sorrowful, or even nostalgic as he remembered the high points of an illustrious career? Not a bit of it. A letter he wrote made it clear he had firmly disliked every moment:

> *As I laid down my baton at the ball … I knew that I had now conducted for the last time, and I cannot describe what feelings came over me in this moment when, after thirty-nine years' work with all its unpleasantness, rancour, troubles, sorrows, deprivations and exertions … I had now reached my goal.*

Eduard Strauss with his
wife, during his tour in the
United States in 1890.

Here was a man as far removed from the traditional image of the swaying Strauss, composer and performer of lovely melodies, as it is possible to be. If his elder brother did not conform to that traditional image, how much further removed from it was his younger brother!

If we take Eduard at his word (and all his writings and utterings seem to confirm it) he had not only been a reluctant musician, but he had not enjoyed any of it. It is possible to argue that to some extent he was responsible for this – he was a difficult man who resented living in his elder brother's shadow, and it was on his shoulders that the rigours, even tedium, of touring fell – but that does not alter the fact that he was not happy in his job.

It is not difficult, then, to envisage the pleasure with which he laid down his baton in New York, and the joy with which he summoned the forty-two players in the Johann Strauss Orchestra the following morning. They must have known what was coming.

Eduard Strauss lived on, alone, for nine more years, in increasingly declining health. He saw the music of the Strauss family slowly fall out of favour, as names such as Franz Lehár, Oskar Straus and John Philip Sousa competed for public attention.

Eduard Strauss suffered a fatal heart attack on the night of 28 December 1916, and died in the presence of his housekeeper. He was eighty-one years of age. His death brought to an end a golden epoch of Viennese music-making, and closed two generations in the most prolific and popular musical family, not just in Vienna but in musical history.

Chapter Twenty-one
A NEW CENTURY AND
A NEW VIENNA

Right

Left: Franz Ferdinand, heir to the Habsburg throne.

Right: Gavrilo Princip, Franz Ferdinand's assassin.

In a grim and infinitely more portentous echo of the assassination of Empress Sisi more than a decade earlier, in June 1914 a group of Serb nationalists slipped into Sarajevo with orders to assassinate Archduke Franz Ferdinand. The ultimate aim of the conspiracy was to break off parts of Serbia from the Austro-Hungarian empire, as part of a wider ambition to restore Serbia to the broader frontiers and greater power it enjoyed in centuries past.

A bizarre, almost unbelievably absurd sequence of events led to a successful assassination. At first they botched it. A bomb thrown at the archduke's car bounced off the hood, exploded under the next car and wounded two officers. But Franz Ferdinand was unharmed and, accompanied by his wife, continued to a morning engagement at the Town Hall.

With typical brashness he interrupted the mayor's speech of welcome with the words: 'Mr Mayor, I came here on a visit and I get bombs thrown at me. It is outrageous.' Only after his wife calmed him down did he allow the mayor to continue with his speech.

The engagement over, the archduke instructed his driver to take him and his wife to the local hospital to visit those who had been injured in the bomb attack. In a single innocent error, which would echo down the years, the driver took a wrong turning and found himself back in the street where the bomb had been thrown, ironically named Franz Josef Strasse.

As it happened, one of the would-be assassins, the Bosnian-Serb Gavrilo Princip, was standing outside a café in the same street, no

doubt bemoaning the failure of the mission. He instantly spotted the archduke's limousine, and must have watched bemused as the driver, realising his mistake, put his foot on the brake, slammed the gear lever into reverse, and tried to back out.

But the gears locked and the engine of the car stalled. It gave Princip exactly the opportunity he needed to carry out the task that had brought him to Sarajevo. He calmly walked towards the stationary car and fired two shots at his – literally – sitting targets.

The archduke's wife Sophie, hit in the abdomen, instinctively covered her husband's body with her own. Franz Ferdinand, bleeding from a wound in the neck, cried out to his wife, 'Sophie darling! Sophie darling! Don't die! Stay alive for our children!' (*'Sopherl! Sopherl! Sterbe nicht! Bleibe am Leben für unsere Kinder!'*)

By the time the limousine arrived at the hospital, both the archduke and his wife were dead, and the history of the world was about to change.

Back in Vienna the old emperor, eighty-three years of age, was once again brought news of the sudden and violent death of a member of his family. Old and frail in mind and body maybe, but he immediately realised the import of what had happened.

First and foremost the heir to the Habsburg throne was dead, the second to die suddenly. What would this mean for the dynasty? On a broader front it was almost inevitable that once Austria issued any kind of ultimatum against Serbia in response, Russia would come to the support of the Serbs, threatening the empire. This meant that

Austria had to mobilise, to protect itself. At least that was what the emperor's ministers persuaded him was beyond question.

But wait, he said, further advice was needed, and he sought it from a ruler who was younger, more in tune with events, with a larger and more efficient army, than him. Kaiser Wilhelm, Emperor of Germany.

The kaiser's response was instant and reassuring. In the event of war with Russia, Germany would enter hostilities on the side of Austria. It was exactly the reassurance Franz Josef sought, but he was under no illusions.

'Now we can no longer turn back. It will be a terrible war,' he said. That judgement was wrong only in the sense of it proving to be a gross understatement.

And what were the people of Vienna doing in the years leading up to these momentous events? They were doing what they had been

doing for decades, doing what came naturally and enjoying the gaiety and laughter that ran in their blood. This was the city that had invented *Gemütlichkeit*.

It is the ability to understand that the key to happiness is the acceptance of what one cannot change. It is the message of *Die Fledermaus*, the single masterwork by Johann Strauss that so perfectly captured the mood of the Viennese and encapsulated it in music.

And so the Viennese were continuing to waltz, to escape into the essentially Viennese world of operetta. Johann Strauss was with them no more, they had lost their Waltz King, but there was another name now receiving their praise and adulation.

This time it was a composer born many miles from Vienna, and even in another country, who settled in Vienna, composed his music there, and became in all but name a Viennese. Franz Lehár might never have earned the sobriquet 'The Waltz King', and his world was more that of operetta than the pure waltz, but he could turn out a composition to stand comparison with those of any of the Strausses.

Relaxing and dancing – quite possibly to the music of the Strausses – in one of the dozens of cafés and dance halls that sprang up in Vienna in the late 18th and early 19th centuries.

In 1902 the Viennese thrilled to his *'Gold and Silver Waltz'*, composed for the Gold and Silver Ball of a member of the aristocracy, and only three years later he produced an operetta whose success came closer to that of *Die Fledermaus* than anything else either he or Johann Strauss wrote: *Die Lustige Witwe*, 'The Merry Widow'.

The era of Johann Strauss was ended; but there were new names and new forms of entertainment on offer. The dance hall had given way to the café, the waltz had yielded to the operetta.

A new generation of Viennese was enjoying life just as their parents and grandparents had before them. They had the same emperor but in other ways they had broken with the past. It was a new century in a multitude of different ways.

Music, though, was still in their blood. It coursed through their veins as it had done for centuries past. The Viennese would still sing and dance, but now it would be to the music of a new generation of composers. And they would, of course, drink champagne for years and years to come. There was, surely, nothing that could take these pleasures away.

And then Gavrilo Princip fired those shots.

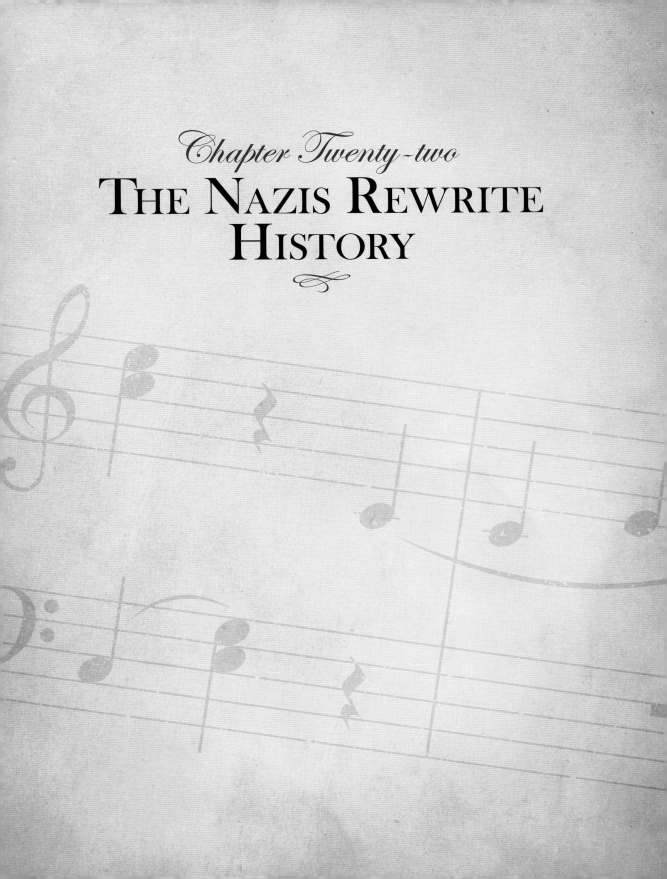

Chapter Twenty-two

THE NAZIS REWRITE HISTORY

During the first half of the twentieth century, the Habsburg empire consigned to history, Franz Josef long dead, having finally been granted his wish at the age of eighty-six, the defeated German kaiser dethroned and in exile in the Netherlands, Europe continued to reverberate to the music of Johann Strauss.

Johann III recovered from his financial woes, put his brief prison sentence behind him, and began to benefit from new technology to make the first wax-cylinder recordings of his uncle's music with his 'Johann Strauss's Vienna Orchestra'.

He toured too. In 1931, taking full advantage of sharing the name of the great composer, he subtly renamed the orchestra and performed at the Royal Albert Hall in London as 'Johann Strauss and his own Viennese orchestra'.

Johann Strauss III produced around thirty compositions, none of them coming close to anything his uncles or father had created. He died suddenly on 9 January 1939 at the age of seventy-two.

Perhaps he was fortunate to die just before the outbreak of the Second World War, for what would happen to the reputation of his family under the Nazis would surely have left him stunned and angry.

***

For the Nazis, keen to claim great German artists as the Aryan ideal – Richard Wagner being the prime example – Johann Strauss the Younger was an obvious candidate. His music was universally popular.

Left

Johann Strauss III, inheritor of a famous name, whose financial improprieties alienated him from his father and landed him in prison.

In June 1939 the Nazi newspaper *Der Stürmer* carried this description of him:

> *The whole world knows Johann Strauss, the Waltz King, with his incomparable melodies. There is hardly any other type of music which is so German and so close to the people as that of the great Waltz King. Johann Strauss is long since dead. He has become immortal.*

Hitler's Minister of Propaganda Joseph Goebbels lost no time in appropriating Strauss to the Nazi cause. But there were two inconveniences, one minor and one very major indeed.

The minor one was that Strauss was not actually German; he was Austrian.[80] This was solved in March 1938 when German troops marched into Vienna and Austria was annexed into the Third Reich, an event known as the *Anschluss*. Almost forty years after his death, Johann Strauss was now as German as someone born in Berlin.

The major problem for the man who in 1938 published 'Ten Principles of German Music Creativity', in which he explicitly called for all good Germans to fight against the infiltration of Jewish music in German culture, was that Johann Strauss had Jewish blood. Not very much – actually not quite enough to make him Jewish under the strict laws brought in by the Nazis themselves – but even a single drop was a drop too many.

It was there in writing for anyone to see. The register of St Stephen's Cathedral recorded the marriage of Johann's great-grandfather on 11 February 1762 thus:

> *Johann Michael Strauss, a respectable man, servant … a baptised Jew, single, born in Ofen, legitimate son of Wolf Strauss and his wife Theresia, both Jewish …*

According to the Nuremberg Laws of 1935, to be classified as German all four grandparents had to be Aryan. One or two grandparents only led to the classification of *Mischling* ('Half-caste'). Three grandparents who were Jewish, or a single parent (of either sex), meant you were Jewish.

---

[80] It seems either the Nazis did not know of his change of nationality to clear the path to his marriage, or discounted it.

Johann Strauss senior was therefore a *Mischling*, while his off-spring were second-class *Mischlings*. This was not 'full-blooded' Jewishness by Nazi rules, and could even be upgraded to 'honorary Aryan' under certain circumstances, and with Hitler's personal approval.

But Goebbels did not want to go down that route. It was essential Johann Strauss the Younger was absolved of any Jewish connection. Goebbels recorded in his diary that Johann was one-eighth Jewish – in fact he was one-sixteenth – but that was one-eighth too much. He thus set in train one of the most bizarre acts of forgery perpetrated by the Third Reich.

The original register of St Stephen's Cathedral, recording great-grandfather Strauss's marriage, and his background, was removed and sent to the Department of Nationality and Race in Berlin, with orders from Goebbels that the offending entry should be carefully taken out, and then returned to Vienna.

One wonders how Goebbels or anyone found time to devote so much energy to the question of the Strauss family's Jewishness, given that they had a war to run, but devote it they did.

In Berlin the entire register was recorded page by page on microfilm, and a copy then produced on vellum, which was then bound in four volumes. Anyone examining the copy and looking for Johann Michael Strauss would find that he was missing. The next entry had been moved up to fill the gap. He had also been deleted from the index, so that the records no longer contained any evidence that the marriage had taken place.

The original, and copies, were returned to Vienna. The first page of volume one of the copies bore an official stamp of the Department of Nationality and Race, and the swastika seal of the Third Reich, certifying that it was an exact copy of the original. It was dated 20 February 1941.

That original, containing the entry for Johann Michael Strauss the Jew, was carefully hidden in the State Archive, well removed from St Stephen's Cathedral. The copies were replaced in the Cathedral.

There is a legend, impossible to verify, that in the spring of 1945, as the Nazis set about destroying Vienna as a farewell gesture, a man ran through the streets of the city clutching the original register. Determined to keep it safe, he secreted it in a deep vault beneath St Stephen's Cathedral. How he obtained it or who he was is unknown.

"Much of the inner city was destroyed, including the house in the Igelgasse where Johann so often sought sanctuary."

Above

The tomb of Emperor Franz Josef, with Empress Elisabeth on the left and Crown Prince Rudolf on the right, closer in death than they ever were in life.

Yet in an extraordinary acknowledgement of just how important she had been to the old man, and the esteem in which his family held her, courtiers at the palace had been given orders to admit her immediately into the private apartments, and then into the simple and austere bedroom where the emperor lay on the plain iron bed on which he had died.

The emperor's daughter, Archduchess Valerie, who had remained close to her father after Empress Sisi's tragic death, embraced her like a mother. Kathi walked to the bed, placed two white roses in the emperor's hands and bent over him, her eyes closed in prayer.

Franz Josef was buried with all the pomp of a great state funeral, sovereigns and princes of the empire converging on Vienna. But Kathi Schratt stayed away. She knew it was not her place to be there.

I expect that Kathi was in some ways grateful that the emperor did not live to see the end of the First World War, the defeat of Germany and Austria, and with it the abolition of the empire he had strived so hard to keep together.

Defeat brought financial hardship and ruin to the aristocratic classes and nobility. Money became worthless almost overnight, banks collapsed, the stock exchange crashed. Kathi was more fortunate than most, in that her assets were mainly in the form of gifts from the emperor and valuable artefacts she had collected over the years.

Soon a steady trickle of these made their way to the auction houses of Vienna, to keep Kathi afloat financially. On one occasion she asked her godson, who was attached to the Austrian Legation in London, to negotiate the sale of some valuable snuffboxes in the hope that Queen Mary might be interested. Apparently word came back from Buckingham Palace that the price was too high.

Those who might have expected Kathi to retire from public life, now that her usefulness at court was at an end, were to be disappointed. She reacquainted herself with her former world of the theatre, and many a young and impecunious actor found himself entertained at her table.

Sunday luncheons at her small house in Hietzing became famous in theatrical circles, with trays and confectionery sent round from Demel, the confectioner in the Kohlmarkt that was the city's best known.[82] There was a cacophony of sound, as boisterous conversation competed with the many stray dogs Kathi had collected and given sanctuary to.

Life in Vienna, once the most sophisticated city in Continental Europe, had changed for ever. Gone was the sumptuousness and grandeur of a capital city of empire, to be replaced by austerity and the shame of a defeated country.

None of this caused Kathi to retreat into obscurity. In her seventies she was still to be seen regularly at the Salzburg Festival, or taking a cure at the spa town of Karlsbad. In 1929, at the age of seventy-six, she boarded an aeroplane for the flight from Zurich to Vienna.

One thing Kathi Schratt did not do, though, which perhaps earns our admiration and frustration in equal measure. In the 1930s journalists beat a path to her door, offering large sums of money in foreign currencies for her memoirs – what we could call today a 'kiss-and-tell'.

---

[82] It still is.

All offers were politely but firmly refused, one such refusal reported and much admired. 'I was never a Pompadour, still less a Maintenon,' she said, in a witty and apt acknowledgement of her role.

Every now and then a sensational article would appear in a magazine, in which she was referred to as 'the emperor's sweetheart', or 'the *gnädige Frau* of Schönbrunn'. She told her friends she never read a word of any of them.

Only once did she react with anger at anything that was printed about her. She was furious when she was told one article said she had accepted a pension from Herr Hitler. She angrily denied it, and when later, in the spring of 1938, Hitler drove in triumph through Vienna after the *Anschluss*, she pulled down the blinds of her windows.

Kathi Schratt died on an April day in 1940. Like the man to whom she had devoted so much of her life, she was eighty-six years of age. Like him too, she died in the middle of a world war and did not live to see Austria defeated.

As for the innermost secrets of an emperor who had ruled for nearly seventy years, whose empire was no more, who had lost his brother, wife, son and nephew to assassination and suicide, whose shoulders bent – literally – under the intolerable weight of matters of state and personal tragedy, Kathi Schratt took them to her grave.

Chapter Twenty-three
ADMIRED BY THE GREATS

was speaking rather begrudgingly when he said, 'A waltz of Johann Strauss is good music in its proper place.'

To say that the music of the Strausses lives on is something of an understatement. There is hardly a capital city in Europe, indeed in the developed world, that does not put on a concert of Strauss music to celebrate New Year.

The most famous of these is the New Year's Concert held in the gilded Musikverein in the city to which the Strauss family belonged, Vienna. The tradition began in the dark days of 1939 – the first such concert was actually held on New Year's Eve of that year, roughly a year and a half after Austria's annexation by Nazi Germany. In fact its origins were severely tainted. The concert was created for the purpose of appeasing and flattering the Nazi occupiers.

That was the first and last time the concert was held on New Year's Eve. There was a two-year hiatus caused by the war, then from 1941 it was held on New Year's Day – perhaps to signify a break with the past and its iniquitous origination – and has been every single year since.

Since 1987 it has become customary to invite a renowned maestro to conduct the concert, and some of the great names in conducting have performed the task – Herbert von Karajan, Carlos Kleiber, Lorin Maazel,[84] Claudio Abbado, Riccardo Muti, Daniel Barenboim, Zubin Mehta, to name but a few – but no one conducted more Vienna New Year concerts than Willi Boskovsky.

Not a conductor, but leader of the Vienna Philharmonic, Boskovsky believed in doing it the way the Strausses themselves did it, and he led the orchestra from the violin for twenty-five consecutive years. I have indelible images in my memory of watching the concert in black and white as a teenager in the 1950s and 1960s, Boskovsky swaying on the podium with his violin under his chin. It was the first time I had heard a Strauss waltz. I was transfixed, and remain so.

Traditionally the conductor conducts without scores, each piece committed to memory, and afterwards, applauded by admiring

---

[84] On one occasion, Maazel put down his baton, lifted his violin, and played the zither solos at the start and end of 'Tales from the Vienna Woods'.

crowds braving the cold of a Viennese New Year's Day, he walks the red carpet from the Musikverein to the Hotel Imperial directly opposite for a celebratory glass of champagne.

Today the concert is beamed live around the world, and is watched by an audience of literally millions. So popular is it that if you wish to attend, your application has to be in by 31 January for the following year's concert, and then tickets are allocated by lottery. Some seats are held by Austrian families and are passed down from generation to generation.

The very first New Year's Concert consisted of music exclusively by Johann Strauss the Younger. Now it includes music by father and all three sons, as well as other composers – mainly Austrian – such as Lanner, Nicolai, von Suppé, even Mozart.

One thing is guaranteed. Two pieces will always be performed, although not in the programme itself but as encores. They are, quite simply, the two best-known compositions ever to come out of Vienna.

Surprising though it may seem, neither *'By the Beautiful Blue Danube'* nor the *'Radetzky March'* were performed in the early New

Acknowledgements

As with my previous book *Beethoven: The Man Revealed*, it was Darren Henley, then Managing Director of Classic FM, who commissioned me to write the story of the Strauss dynasty and the city of Vienna in which father and sons lived. My gratitude to him is boundless, and I wish him every success in his new role as Chief Executive of Arts Council, England.

Once again, I am grateful to Lorne Forsyth, Chairman of Elliott & Thompson, Classic FM's publisher, for his support throughout, and to my editor Olivia Bays, Director at Elliott & Thompson. Olivia is a superb editor and a joy to work with. I set Pippa Crane, Senior Editor at Elliott & Thompson, a Herculean task in tracking down the best part of a hundred illustrations and the book is infinitely better for her efforts.

The eagle eyes of copyeditor Jill Burrows corrected several inconsistencies in the manuscript and improved some infelicities of style, and James Collins designed a book that far outshone my expectations, as he did with *Beethoven*.

To see the two books side by side on my shelf, I confess rather immodestly, causes me some pride.

Picture Credits